T0239141

Migrating to Swift from Android

Sean Liao

Apress®

Migrating to Swift from Android

ISBN-13 (pbk): 978-1-4842-0437-5

ISBN-13 (electronic): 978-1-4842-0436-8

Trademarked names, logos, and images may appear in this book. Rather than use a trademark symbol with every occurrence of a trademarked name, logo, or image we use the names, logos, and images only in an editorial fashion and to the benefit of the trademark owner, with no intention of infringement of the trademark.

The use in this publication of trade names, trademarks, service marks, and similar terms, even if they are not identified as such, is not to be taken as an expression of opinion as to whether or not they are subject to proprietary rights.

While the advice and information in this book are believed to be true and accurate at the date of publication, neither the authors nor the editors nor the publisher can accept any legal responsibility for any errors or omissions that may be made. The publisher makes no warranty, express or implied, with respect to the material contained herein.

Publisher: Heinz Weinheimer
Lead Editor: Steve Anglin
Development Editor: Matthew Moodie
Technical Reviewer: Alex Decker
Editorial Board: Steve Anglin, Ewan Buckingham, Gary Cornell, Louise Corrigan,
    James T. DeWolf, Jonathan Gennick, Robert Hutchinson, Michelle Lowman,
    James Markham, Matthew Moodie, Jeff Olson, Jeffrey Pepper, Douglas Pundick,
    Ben Renow-Clarke, Dominic Shakeshaft, Gwenan Spearing, Steve Weiss
Coordinating Editor: Anamika Panchoo
Copy Editor: James M. Fraleigh
Compositor: SPi Global
Indexer: SPi Global
Artist: SPi Global
Cover Designer: Anna Ishchenko

Distributed to the book trade worldwide by Springer Science+Business Media New York, 233 Spring Street, 6th Floor, New York, NY 10013. Phone 1-800-SPRINGER, fax (201) 348-4505, e-mail orders-ny@springer-sbm.com, or visit www.springeronline.com. Apress Media, LLC is a California LLC and the sole member (owner) is Springer Science + Business Media Finance Inc (SSBM Finance Inc). SSBM Finance Inc is a Delaware corporation.

For information on translations, please e-mail rights@apress.com, or visit www.apress.com.

Apress and friends of ED books may be purchased in bulk for academic, corporate, or promotional use. eBook versions and licenses are also available for most titles. For more information, reference our Special Bulk Sales–eBook Licensing web page at www.apress.com/bulk-sales.

Any source code or other supplementary material referenced by the author in this text is available to readers at www.apress.com. For detailed information about how to locate your book's source code, go to www.apress.com/source-code/.

Contents at a Glance

Contents

About the Author

Sean Liao (PMP®) started his first mobile app on a PalmOS PDA app in 2000. He hasn't missed any major mobile evolutions. He has written mobile code for PalmOS, JavaME, Microsoft .NET CF, and BlackBerry, and he also has some Nokia Symbian experience. He has been a seasoned Java solution architect since 1998.

In 2009, Sean started programming in iOS, and then began programming in Android the same year by following the same porting strategy, based on years of hands-on mobile programming experience. Currently, Sean is primarily engaged in creating iOS apps and porting them to Android as a bonus.

About the Technical Reviewer

Alex Decker is a mobile application developer specializing in enterprise applications. He graduated from the University of Illinois and currently lives with his wife in California.

Acknowledgments

Looking back on the journey of this book-writing experience, I realize clearly now that I never would have started it without the encouragement from my lovely wife, Lily, and I never would have completed it without her support. My two little princesses, Megan and Melanie, also really motivated me. As I was writing the book they would come by repeatedly to ask me silly questions, like, "Can I help you, Daddy? Daddy, will the book be this thick? Daddy, can your book be my bedtime story? Will you play with me more after you finish it?"

I knew I would never give up.

Special thanks to my publisher, who had faith in this topic, and the editors, who never stopped making the book better. Their professional services and guidance are unparalleled. I am really grateful to have had the Apress publishing and editorial teams with me at all times.

Introduction

In 2000, I started my first PalmOS mobile app for an inventory-tracking project. The initial project was a full-staffed team effort that consisted of mobile developers, SAP consultants, supply-chain subject matter experts, middleware developers, QA testers, architects, business sponsors, and so forth. JavaME came up strong in 2002, followed by Pocket PC/Windows Mobile. I did several mobile projects in which I converted mobile apps to the Pocket PC platform by blindly translating JavaME code to C# .NETCF mobile code. These "translation" efforts prolonged the whole product life cycle. The project achieved higher ROI as the product life extended, because the extra cost of translating mobile code was surprisingly low. Ever since then, I have been translating front-end mobile apps among JavaME, BlackBerry, and Windows Mobile platforms.

In early 2009, by repeating the same porting process, I created my first iOS app by translating a Windows mobile app. That started my iOS programming journey, and later it was a no-brainer for me to try porting to Android. Most mobile apps are platform agnostic. When you have the whole solution completed for either iOS or Android, all the business and technical issues have been verified and the other deliverables and project artifacts are already reusable. It would be a waste not to port it to the other platform. Earlier this year, I wrote my first book, *Migrating to Android for iOS Developers*, to share my beliefs and experiences. After Swift was introduced at Worldwide Developers Conference (WWDC) 2014, I decided to write this book because the similarity between Java and Swift makes the porting method even easier while the same ROI analysis remains true.

The primary objective of this book is to help experienced Android developers leap into native iOS–Swift mobile development. It is easier than you think, and this book will make it even easier with Android analogies and mapping guidelines. You can immediately translate common mobile use cases to iOS.

Who Is This Book For?

This book is specifically written for Android developers who want to take advantage of their mobile knowledge and make mobile applications available on the iOS mobile platform. The book will show you the common iOS programming subjects and frameworks using your familiar Android vocabularies without lengthy explanations, because you already know these mobile subjects from being an Android developer.

How This Book Is Organized

In Part I, you will get the iOS Xcode integrated development environment (IDE) up and running in no time. You will be guided in creating tutorial projects that will become your porting sample projects. I believe this is the best way for you to get hands-on experience while learning programming topics.

Part II of this book shows you how to plan and structure your iOS apps: by creating a storyboard and breaking the app into model-view-controller (MVC) classes. You will be able to reuse most of the existing software artifacts and design the rest from their Android counterparts. The common mobile topics are followed, including user interface, managing data, and networking with remote services. After you finish Part II, you will be able to create simple but meaningful iOS apps with rich UI components, and to handle common CRUD (create, read, update, delete) operations locally and remotely.

Last, Part III walks you through a case study that ports a complete iOS app to Android. It recaps how to use mapping guidelines from the topics in Part II. You can also use the book's table of contents to help find the porting guidelines as needed.

When you complete this journey, you will be able to use Xcode and Swift to effectively port your existing Android apps to iOS.

Prepare Your Tools

A handy tool makes a handy person. This is very true for creating software, too. Xcode is the integrated development environment (IDE) for writing, compiling, debugging, and building code for iOS application development. The first part of the chapter walks you through the installation and steps for getting it up and running. All the topics in this book come with sample code. You will need to use Xcode to learn from these sample projects, and you will use Xcode to create world-class iOS apps, too.

For iOS programming, Swift is the latest and greatest programming language released for iOS 8. The chapters in this part will give you enough knowledge to read and write the sample code in Swift. You will find learning Swift a very natural extension from your use of Java, and you will surely feel comfortable using the code from this book as your own code.

Chapter 1

Setting Up the Development Environment

It is more fun to see apps run than to read the source code, and you cannot get hands-on programming experience by just reading books. Let's get the development environment up and running first so you can use it—and learn Swift programming for iOS along the way.

Xcode and the iOS SDK

ANDROID ANALOGY

The Android Developer Tools (ADT plug-in for Eclipse or Android Studio.

Xcode is the complete toolset for building iOS apps. It is an integrated development environment (IDE) that helps you build, test, debug, and package your iOS apps. It is free but you must have an Intel-based Mac running Mac OS X Mavericks or later. You will use the latest Xcode, version 6, throughout this book.

Installing from the Mac App Store

Xcode is distributed in the Mac App Store, which takes care of the download and install for you. With a single click to start the download and installation of Xcode, you get the compilers, code editor, iOS SDK, debugger, device emulators, and everything you need to create iOS apps. Figure 1-1 shows Xcode in the Mac App Store app.

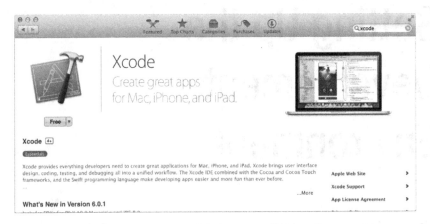

Figure 1-1. Xcode in Mac App Store

All you need to do is install the latest Xcode from the Mac App Store. After completing the installation, go ahead and launch Xcode from the **Applications** folder. Keep it in the Mac OS Dock so that you can launch it at any time.

The first time you launch Xcode, it immediately prompts you to install the required components (see Figure 1-2). Click **Install** to complete the Xcode installation.

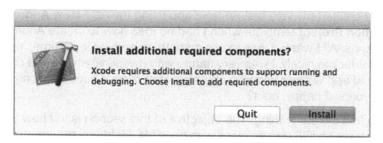

Figure 1-2. Install the required components

After the required components are installed, you should see the screenshot in Figure 1-3. Your iOS IDE, Xcode, is ready!

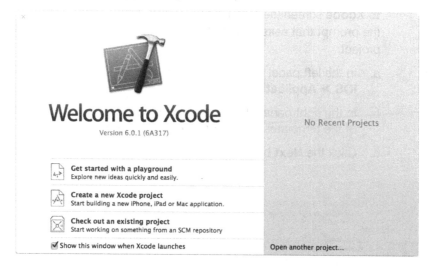

Figure 1-3. Welcome to Xcode

Create an iOS Project Using the Template

ANDROID ANALOGY

New Android Application Project template in ADT.

You've got the right tool; now, wouldn't you like to see some real action—like creating an iOS app and seeing it run? I'd like that, too! You want to do this to ensure your IDE is working properly as well.

I actually created my very first Android app using the ADT **New Android Application Project** template when I had no idea how to create Android mobile apps. All I wanted was to see something running in no time. Yep, ADT did it for me nicely. I was very happy with myself when I felt I'd created an Android app without knowing anything! Hey, there's nothing wrong with making yourself happy, right?

Xcode offers the same thing. The objective of this section is to show you how to create an iOS app as quickly as possible. Hold any programming questions so you can finish the project as fast as you can. For now, complete the following steps:

1. Launch Xcode if you haven't launched it yet.

2. Select **Create a new Xcode project** from the **Welcome to Xcode** screen (see Figure 1-3). Figure 1-4 shows the prompt that asks you to choose a template for your project:

    a. In the left panel of Figure 1-4, select **iOS ➤ Application**.

    b. In the right panel of Figure 1-4, you may choose any of the templates. Just for fun, choose **Game**.

    c. Click the **Next** button.

Figure 1-4. Choose a template

3. Figure 1-5 depicts the basic project info that requires you to fill in the following:

    a. *Product Name*: This is the app name. Name your project LessonOne.

    b. *Organization Name*: Optional; for example, **Your organization** or any name you choose.

    c. *Organization Identifier*: Together with the product name, the *organization identifier* should uniquely identify your app. Reverse domain name is recommended (e.g., com.yourdomain.xxx).

    d. *Language*, *Game Technology*, and *Device*: You don't need to change these settings.

    e. Click the **Next** button when done.

    f. Select a folder in which to save your LessonOne project.

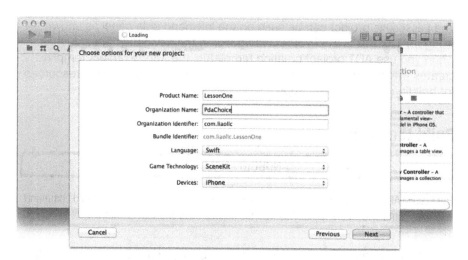

Figure 1-5. iOS project options

That is it! You just created an iOS project, the LessonOne project as shown in Figure 1-6.

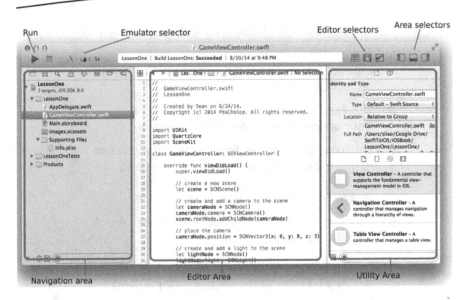

Run   Emulator selector   Editor selectors   Area selectors

Navigation area   Editor Area   Utility Area

Figure 1-6. LessonOne project in Xcode Project Navigator

The LessonOne project can be seen on the left-hand side panel as shown in Figure 1-6; this is the **Project Navigator** in the navigation area. Just as when you use ADT project creation templates, the Xcode project template creates the project folder, the application source code, and all the resources for building the LessonOne apps.

Build the Project

ANDROID ANALOGY

The Eclipse ADT Build action keyboard shortcut on the Mac is the same as the build command in Xcode: Command+B (⌘+B). In Windows the Eclipse build shortcut is Control+B.

To build and compile the Xcode project, use the Build action, which is located in the Xcode menubar ➤ **Product** ➤ **Build** (or ⌘+B). You will get used to using the ⌘+B keyboard shortcut a lot because Xcode doesn't automatically build your code, unlike Eclipse ADT, which builds it automatically by default.

Launch the App

The LessonOne project should have no errors. You can launch the app and see it run on an iOS emulator. The emulator is a very important piece of any IDE. Unlike ADT, there is no need to mess with something like AVD Manager to create an emulator. All the emulators are right there in Xcode and you can launch the LessonOne project onto the selected device, including the iOS emulator, with a click on the triangle button in the upper left corner as shown in Figure 1-6.

Alternatively, you may use an Xcode keyboard shortcut key for the Run action, Command+R (⌘+R), to launch the app. You should see your LessonOne app running on the iPhone emulator as shown in Figure 1-7.

Figure 1-7. LessonOne app in Emulator

Play with the app, and then select other emulators from the device emulator selector (see the pointer in Figure 1-6). A mouse-click event on an emulator is equivalent to a touch event, and three-finger movement on the trackpad is equivalent to touch-drag on a physical iOS screen. If you don't have a particular device yet, definitely play with the emulator to get familiar with the emulated iOS devices.

> **Tip**   To change to landscape or portrait orientation, press ⌘+left arrow or right arrow to rotate the emulator.

The iOS emulators are way better than AVD—very robust and responsive, and they behave just like real devices. For learning Swift programming for iOS, the emulator actually is better, as iOS developers use emulators much more frequently than Android developers. In this book, you are not required to run apps on a physical iOS device; for that you would need to be a registered iOS developer and an iOS device. You can save the $99 iOS developer membership fee until you are ready to submit your first app to the App Store or if your app requires certain features not available in the emulator (e.g., the camera or certain sensors). For now, if your app is launched and running on an iOS emulator, your mission is completed!

Summary

By installing Xcode 6, you immediately have a fully functional IDE ready to create iOS apps without hassle. This chapter walked you through the basic project-creation tasks in Xcode 6, using an iOS project template to start your first iOS project. This chapter also showed you how to build and run your iOS app in iOS emulators. You haven't written any code yet, but your tool is working and verified. You will learn more and gain hands-on programming experience from the guided exercises in the following chapters.

Chapter **2**

iOS Programming Basics

Creating mobile apps for both iOS and Android is fun and rewarding. With Xcode in place, you are ready to write code, build, and run iOS apps now. Objective-C had been the primary programming language for iOS apps until Swift was officially announced at the 2014 Apple Worldwide Developers Conference. If you're just starting to learn iOS programming, you should go with Swift because there is no reason to choose the old way and miss the latest and great features. Your next steps should be learning the fundamentals of the following:

- The Swift programming language
- The anatomy of the iOS project and the Xcode storyboard editor

The purpose of this chapter is to get you comfortable with reading the Swift code in this book. To achieve this goal, you will be creating a HelloSwift project while learning **Swift programming language** highlights.

You will create another Xcode iOS project in the second part of the chapter. All iOS apps have a user interface (UI). You normally start by creating the UI using the most important Xcode tool, **Storyboard Editor,** which draws the UI widgets and components and connects them to your code. You also will see the typical iOS project structures and components while creating this iOS app. You may not need to understand everything about the iOS framework in the beginning, but the first storyboard lesson should be "just enough" for you to feel the different programming paradigm. Later, the materials in Chapters 3 and 4 continue with step-by-step instructions for common programming tasks and framework topics. Follow these mapping instructions, and the ideas will more easily stick with you as you get a broader picture of the whole app.

The Swift Language in a Nutshell

Swift, the newest programming language for creating iOS apps, has many similar rules and aspects of language syntax to Java. I am very confident that learning the Swift language won't be the highest hurdle for you; Java or C# developers will pick up Swift code naturally. Just to give you a quick preview, Table 2-1 depicts a quick Java-to-Swift comparison:

Table 2-1. Java-to-Swift Language Syntax Comparison in an Absolute Nutshell

Java	Swift
`import packagename.Xyz;`	**import** `framework`
`class Xyz extends SomeClass`	**class** `Xyz : SomeClass`
`interface Abc`	**protocol** `Abc`
`class Xyz extends SomeClass implements Abc`	`class Xyz: SomeClass, Abc`
`int mProperty;`	**var** `mProperty :` **Int**
`Xyz() // constructor`	`init()`
`Xyz obj = new Xyz();`	`var obj : Xyz = Xyz()`
`void doWork(String arg)`	**func** `doWork (arg: String) ->` Void
`obj.doWork(arg);`	`obj.doWork(arg)`
`Access Modifier: private vs. public`	**private** vs. **public**

Swift also defines **file** and the **module** access control: private, public, and internal. Although they have different meanings from their Java counterparts, if you define each class in each own file, the private/public access controls can be used the same way. The default internal access control is also public to any file in the same project, but is not visible when being imported to other projects. The Swift internal control is more useful for creating framework projects as opposed to app modules.

HelloSwift with Xcode

Instead of my describing the uses and syntax rules in a formal way, you are going to create a HelloSwift Xcode project and write the code listing from Table 2-1 yourself. You will also perform the following common Xcode programming tasks: create a class, build and run a project, and use the debugger.

Create a Swift Command-Line Project

Let's create a command-line Swift program, because it is really simple and you can focus on the Swift language subjects without being sidetracked by other questions.

Follow these instructions to proceed:

1. Launch Xcode 6 if it is not running. You should see the **Welcome to Xcode** launch screen as shown in Figure 1-3. Select **Create a new Xcode Project** (see Figure 1-3). Alternatively, you may do the same by selecting **File ➤ Project...** from the Xcode menu bar.

2. Choose **OS X ➤ Application ➤ Command Line Tool** as shown in the **Choose a template for your new project** screen (see Figure 2-1).

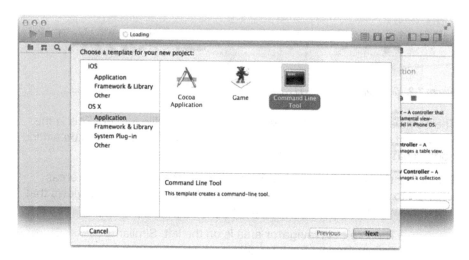

Figure 2-1. Choosing an Xcode template

3. Follow the same on-screen instruction that you used to create the LessonOne project (see Chapter 1, "Create an iOS Project Using the Template") to finish creating the new project with the template:

    a. *Product Name*: HelloSwift

    b. *Organization Name*: for example, PdaChoice

    c. *Organization Identifier*: for example, com.liaollc

    d. Language: Swift

    e.   Click the **Next** button when done.

    f.   Select a folder in which to save your HelloSwift project.

The HelloSwift project appears in the **Project Navigator** area (see Figure 2-2).

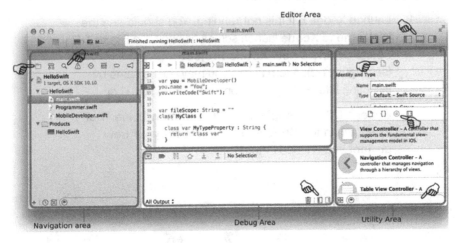

Figure 2-2. *Creating the HelloSwift project*

The command-line template creates the main.swift file for you. This is the entry point of the program, just like the main(...) in Java. You will be writing code in main.swift to demonstrate common object-oriented code.

Figure 2-2 shows that the typical Xcode workspace contains three areas from left to right and a top toolbar. Inside each area, there are subviews that you may switch to using the selector bars.

- The **Project Navigator** area is on the left. Similar to Eclipse Project Explorer, this is where you can see the whole project structure and select the file that you want to edit. There are other views in this area; for example, you can enable Search view by selecting the Search icon in the selector bar.

- The **Source Editor** area in the middle shows the selected file in its editor, in which you can edit the file, writing your code or modifying project settings depending on the file selected. The **Console** and **Variable** views are inside the **Debug** area. Most likely you will want to show them during debugging sessions. You can hide or show them by clicking the toggle buttons on the top and bottom toolbars.

■ The **Utility** area on the right contains several **Inspector** views that allow you edit attributes of the whole file or the item selected in the **Source Editor**. Depending on the type of files you select, different types of Inspectors will be available in the top selector bar. For example, you will have more Inspectors showing in the selector bar if you are editing a screen or UI widgets. The bottom of the area is called **Libraries**. Use the selector bar to select one of the Library views. You can drag and drop items from **Libraries** to the appropriate editor to visually modify file content. You will use **Object Library** a lot to compose UIs visually.

Click on any of the icons on the selector bars, or hover your mouse over the pointer in Figure 2-2, to see the hover text tips in the workspace, to get yourself familiar with Xcode workspace. The subviews appear more condensed than those in Eclipse, but essentially Xcode is a tool for the same purpose: editing project files and compiling, building, debugging, and running the executables. You will use it repeatedly throughout the book.

Create a Swift Class

To create a new Swift class, you can create it in the existing `main.swift` file, or follow the Java convention to create it in its own file as shown in the following steps:

4. Expand the newly created `HelloSwift` project, right-click the `HelloSwift` folder to bring up the folder context menu (see Figure 2-3), and select **New File...**

    a. Choose **iOS ➤ Source** from the left panel and select **Swift File** from the right panel in the **Choose a template for your new file** screen.

    b. Save the file and name it `MobileDeveloper.swift`. The file should appear in your project.

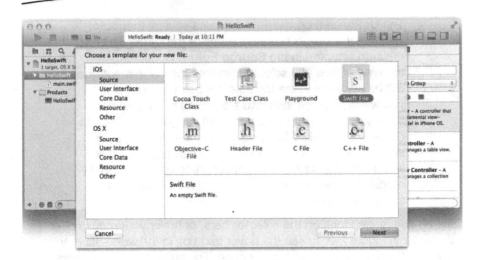

Figure 2-3. Create a Swift class from the folder context menu

5. Enter the code in Listing 2-1 in the MobileDeveloper.swift file to create the MobileDeveloper Swift class.

Listing 2-1. Declare MobileDeveloper Class

```
class MobileDeveloper {

}
```

Note   Unlike Java, a Swift class doesn't implicitly inherit from any class. It can be the base class on its own.

6. Create a property called name by declaring a variable inside the class (see Listing 2-2). This is called a **stored property** in Swift, where the variable type is inferred by the assigned value (known as **type inference** in Swift).

Listing 2-2. Stored Property in Swift

```
class MobileDeveloper {
    var name  = "" // var type is String inferred by the value
}
```

> **Note**   Semicolon (;) is optional for terminating a statement.

Create a Swift Protocol

JAVA ANALOGY

The Java interface defines object obligations.

In object-oriented programming (OOP), it is important to define a set of behaviors that are expected of certain objects. In Java, you declare an **interface**; in Swift, you declare a **protocol**.

Create a Swift protocol called `Programmer` by doing the following:

1. Right-click the `HelloSwift` folder to create the `Programmer.swift` file.

2. In **Source Editor**, create the `Programmer` protocol with a method, `writeCode(...)` as shown in Listing 2-3.

   Listing 2-3. Declare the `Programmer` Protocol

   ```
   protocol Programmer {
     func writeCode(arg: String) -> Void
   }
   ```

Implement the Protocol

JAVA ANALOGY

Implement a Java interface.

To conform to the expected behavior defined in a Swift protocol, the tagged class must implement the methods defined in the protocol. To make the `MobileDeveloper` class implement the `Programmer` protocol, do the following:

1. Modify `MobileDeveloper.swift` and declare the `MobileDeveloper` class to implement the `Programmer` protocol as shown in Listing 2-4.

   Listing 2-4. Conform to `MobileDeveloper` Protocol

   ```
   class MobileDeveloper : Programmer {
     ...
   }
   ```

> **Note**   If the Swift class already has a superclass, list the superclass name before any protocols it adopts, followed by a comma (,)—for example, `class MobileDeveloper : Person, Programmer`

2. Provide the `writeCode(...)` method implementation body, as shown in Listing 2-5.

Listing 2-5. Method Body

```
class MobileDeveloper: Programmer {
    ...
    func writeCode(arg: String) -> Void {
      println("\(self.name) wrote: Hello, \(arg)")
    }
}
```

> **Note**   `\(self.name)` is evaluated first inside the quoted `String` literal.

Use the Swift Instance

JAVA ANALOGY

```
Programmer you = new MobileDeveloper();
you.setName("You");
you.writeCode("Java");
```

You have created a Swift `MobileDeveloper` class and implemented the `Programmer` obligations, in pretty much the same way you normally do in Java except with minor syntax differences. To use the class, it is the same as Java in principle, calling a method defined in the receiver from the sender. Modify `HelloSwift/main.swift` as shown in Listing 2-6.

Listing 2-6. Swift Entry main.swift

```
var you = MobileDeveloper()
you.name = "You";
you.writeCode("Java");
```

Xcode Debugger

Knowing how to use the debugger when creating software can make a big difference in your productivity. Do the following to see the common debugging tasks in the Xcode debugger:

1. To set a **breakpoint**, click on the line number in the Xcode code editor. Figure 2-4 depicts a breakpoint that was set in the main.swift file.

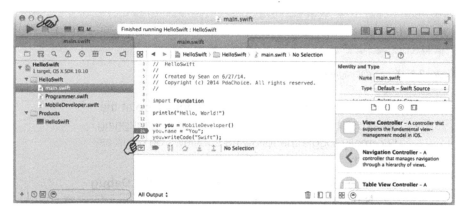

Figure 2-4. Breakpoint

> **Note**   To turn on line numbers in Xcode editors, go to the Xcode top menu bar and select **Xcode ➤ Preferences... ➤ Text Editing ➤ Show Line Numbers**. There are other handy settings there that you may want to look at (e.g., shortcut keys are defined under **Key Binding**).

2. To run the HelloSwift project, click the triangle-shaped **Run** button in the upper left corner, or press ⌘+R (see Figure 2-5).

Figure 2-5. Xcode debugging

3. The Swift program should start and then stop at the breakpoint as shown in Figure 2-5. While debugging, I normally toggle the following subviews on or off as needed:

    a. Hide the **Navigation** area or switch to the **Debug Navigator** to view threads.

    b. Show the **Debug** area with debug toolbar, **Variable**, and **Console** views.

    c. Hide the **Utility** Area.

Stack Trace, **Variables Inspector**, **Output Console**, and the **Debug** toolbar have a similar look and feel in most IDEs, including Xcode and Eclipse.

This completes your HelloSwift application exercise. As you follow through the iOS projects in this book, you will discover more productivity tips in the Xcode IDE.

More About the Swift Language

A lot of Java syntax and conventional coding approaches would work just fine in Swift. However, Swift does have some pretty neat features of its own, so it's worth taking a quick look at them now.

To go through this section, it is best to use the new Xcode feature called **Playgrounds**. Launch Xcode and select **Get Started with a playground**. You can write any code snippets you want and see the result or syntax errors immediately. Figure 2-6 depicts the Playground: you write code in the left panel and the right panel renders the result immediately.

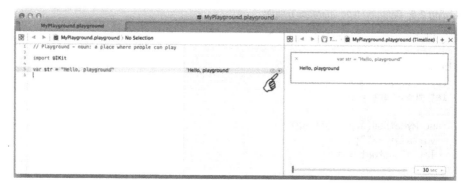

Figure 2-6. Xcode Playground

JAVA ANALOGY

Java scratchpad.

Variables and Constants

You declare a variable using the var keyword, and you use let to declare constants. While Java variables are always defined within the enclosing brackets, Swift variables are global if defined not within enclosing brackets. The following code snippet (see Listing 2-7) depicts usage of Swift variables:

Listing 2-7. Common variables usages

```
var GlobalVar : String = "Global Variable"; // global scope

class MyClass {
  var mProperty : String = ""; // class scope
  let mConstant : Int = 0; // constant

  func myMethod(arg : String) {
    var aVar : String = ""; // local variable in method scope
    let aConstant = 1;
  }
}
```

Type Safety and Type Inference

Both Java and Swift are type-safe languages. Any variable must be declared with a type; the compiler will help flag any mismatched types. In Swift, if the type can be inferred by its value, you don't need to explicitly declare the type. Listing 2-8 is essentially exactly the same as Listing 2-7. The Swift type inference feature encourages developers to assign initial values that reduce the common errors from uninitialized data.

Listing 2-8. Common type inference usages

```
var GlobalVar = "Global Variable"

class MyClass {
  var mProperty = ""
  let mConstant = 0

  func myMethod(arg : String) {
    var aVar = "";
    let aConstant = 1
  }
}
```

Optional Variable

The optional variables are declared with the type and a postfixed question mark (?), called optional type. This indicates the value it contains may be absent (nil, equivalent to null in Java) for the intended type. For example, Listing 2-9 depicts the difference in Swift and Java for converting a string to an integer.

Listing 2-9. Optional Type in Swift vs. Handle Exception in Java

```
////// Java NumberFormatException
String intStr = "123"; // or "xYz"
int myInt;
try {
  myInt = Integer.parseInt("234");
} catch (NumberFormatException e) {
  myInt = Integer.MAX_VALUE;
}

////// Swift Optional Int
var intStr = "123"
var myInt : Int? = intStr.toInt() // myInt can be nil
```

Optionals make the Swift language more type safe and more robust by encouraging developers to understand whether the variable can be absent. Listing 2-10 demonstrates two practical Swift optional usages:

- Forced Unwrapping, which uses a postfixed exclamation pointer (!)

- Optional Binding

Listing 2-10. Swift Optional Int

```
var intStr = "123"
var myOptionalInt : Int? = intStr.toInt() // Optional Int
if myOptionalInt != nil {
  var myInt = myOptionalInt! // Unwrap Int? to Int
  println("unwrapped Int: \(myInt)")
}

// optional binding used in if and while local scope.
if var myInt = intStr.toInt() {
  // myInt is auto unwrapped
  println("unwrapped and local scope: \(myInt)")
}
```

Implicitly Unwrapped Optionals

For the situations where a variable will always have a value after the value is set, you declare the variable as Implicitly Unwrapped Optional postfixed with ! instead of ?. For example: `var delegate: MyDelegate!`

Any of the Optionals usages described earlier are applicable here. You treat it as Optionals but you don't need to force unwrapping it. You commonly see this usage in the iOS framework for properties that are initialized somewhere else (i.e., by the caller). Particularly, iOS frameworks embed delegate properties everywhere. These delegates are declared as Implicitly Unwrapped Optionals but their values are typically assigned by the caller. As another example, UI widgets are normally drawn in the Storyboard editor and connect to your code as `IBOutlet` properties. These `IBOutlet` properties are declared as Implicitly Unwrapped Optionals. I just wanted to give you a quick heads up for now because you will see these usages frequently later in this book.

Tuples

Tuples group multiple values into a single compound value. This seems to have been the useful feature that Java developers (as well as those using C#, Objective-C, C/C++, etc.) have been looking for. For example, you can pass or return a value without creating a class or a struct (structs are also supported in Swift). Listing 2-11 shows the most common tuple usages.

Listing 2-11. Common Tuple Usages

```
var xyz  = (x: 0, y: 0, z: 0)
println("xyz \(xyz) x is: \(xyz.x)\ty is: \(xyz.y)\tz is: \(xyz.z)")

// or decompose tuples
var xy : (Int, Int) = (1, 1) // or simply var xy = (1, 1)
var (a, b) = xy
println("xy \(xy) x is: \(a)\ty is: \(b)")
```

```
func httpResponse() -> (rc: Int, status: String) {
  return (200, "OK")
}

var resp = httpResponse()
println("resp is: \(resp.rc)\t\(resp.status)")
```

Collections

JAVA ANALOGY

`java.lang.ArrayList` and `HashMap`.

Array and `Dictionary` are the two Swift collections. Listing 2-12 shows the common usages, which include the following:

- Initialization

- Access and modify elements using subscript syntax

- Common collection APIs

Listing 2-12. Common Array and Dictionary usages

```
// collections
var emptyArray = Array<String>() // or [String]()
var emptyDict = Dictionary<Int, String>() // [Int: String]()
var colors = ["red", "green", "blue"]
var colorDictionary = ["r" : "red", "g" : "green", "b" : "blue"]
colors.append("alpha") // or: colors += "alpha"
colorDictionary["a"] = colors[3]
colors.insert("pink", atIndex: 2)
colors.removeAtIndex(2)
println(colors.isEmpty ? "empty" : "\(colors.count)")
```

Constant `Dictionary` or `Array` is immutable, meaning it is not allowed to add or remove elements, nor modify existing items. On the other hand, variable `Dictionary` or `Array` is mutable.

Control Flow

Similar to Java, in Swift you use `if` and `switch` to make conditionals, and use `for-in`, `for`, `while`, and `do-while` to make loops. Parentheses around the condition or loop variable are optional. Braces around the body are required. Listing 2-13 demonstrates the following common control flow usages:

- for-loop
- for-in
- while-loop

Listing 2-13. Control Flows

```
for (var idx = 0; idx < 10; idx++) { // optional parenthesis
  println("for-loop: \(idx)")
}

for item in [1,2,3,4,5] { // or for item in 1...5
  println("for-in: \(item)")
}
for c in "HelloSwift" { // loop thru characters
  print(c)
}

for (key, value) in colorDictionary {
  println("for-in dictionary:\(key) - \(value)")
}

// while-loop, or do-while that run at least once
var idx = 0
while idx < colors.count {
  println("while-loop:  \(colors[idx])")
  idx++
}
```

Switch

In Swift, the **switch cases** can be any types in addition to int primitive data. Listing 2-14 shows the following improved control flow switch usages in Swift:

- Combined cases and always break implicitly
- Cases with ranges
- Cases with tuples

Listing 2-14. Improved Switch

```
var condition = "red"
switch condition {
case "red", "green", "blue": // combined cases
  println("\(condition) is a prime color")
  // always break implicitly (no follow thru)
```

```
case "RED", "GREEN", "BLUE":
  println("\(condition) is a prime color in uppercase")
default: // not optional anymore
  println("\(condition) is not prime color")
}

var range = 9 // by range
switch range {
case 0:
  println("zero")
case 0...9:
  println("one-digit number")
case 10...99:
  println("two-digit number")
case 10...999: // first hit first
  println("three-digit number")
default:
  println("four or more digits")
}

var coord = (0, 1)
switch coord { // by tuples
case (0...Int.max, 0...Int.max):
  println("1st quad")
case (Int.min...0, 0...Int.max):
  println("2nd quad")
case (Int.min...0, Int.min...0):
  println("3rd quad")
case (0...Int.max, Int.min...0):
  println("4th quad")
default:
  println("on axis")
}
```

A switch can bind the matched value within its local scope. You can specify a where clause to test the condition, too. Listing 2-15 demonstrates both value bindings.

Listing 2-15. Temporary Value Binding and Using where Clause

```
var rect = (10, 10)
switch rect {
case let (w, h) where w == h:
  println("\((w, h)) is a square")
default:
  println("rectangle but not square")
}
```

Enumerations

You use enum to define a common type for a group of related values. After the enumeration is defined, you use it just as a Swift type that is type safe. Listing 2-16 shows the following common enum usages:

- Enum with or without raw values

- Enum associated with values

Listing 2-16. Common Enum usages

```
enum DayOfWeek { // raw value is optional
  case SUNDAY, MONDAY, TUESDAY, WEDNESDAY,
  THURSDAY, FRIDAY, SATURDAY
}

var aDay = DayOfWeek.SUNDAY
switch aDay {
case DayOfWeek.SATURDAY, DayOfWeek.SUNDAY:
  println("\(aDay) is weekend")
default:
  println("\(aDay) is weekday")
}

enum DayOfWeek2 :  String { // assign raw value
  case SUNDAY = "Sun", MONDAY = "Mon", TUESDAY = "Tue",
  WEDNESDAY = "Wed", THURSDAY = "Thu", FRIDAY = "Fri", SATURDAY = "Sat"
}

var aDay2 = DayOfWeek2.SUNDAY
switch aDay2 {
case DayOfWeek2.SATURDAY, DayOfWeek2.SUNDAY:
  println("\(aDay2.rawValue) is weekend")
default:
  println("\(aDay2.rawValue) is weekday")
}

// associated values
enum Color {
  case RGB(Int, Int, Int)
  case HSB(Float, Float, Float)
}

var aColor = Color.RGB(255, 0, 0)
switch aColor {
case var Color.RGB(r, g, b):
  println("R: \(r) G: \(g) B: \(b) ")
default:
  println("")
}
```

Functions

Swift functions are declared with the `func` keyword. Unlike Java methods, the parameter and return type are declared after the type name. Here are the typical Swift function usages you most likely will encounter (see Listing 2-17):

- *Tuples*: You can return multiple values without creating a `struct` or `class` (see Listing 2-11).

- *External parameter names*: You should treat external parameter names as part of the function signature. All of the iOS Objective-C SDK APIs are ported to Swift with external parameter names.

- *Default parameter values*: Not only does this feature provide a default value, but it also makes method overloading easier in many situations, as opposed to method chaining.

- *Variadic parameters*: Variable length of the method parameters without using `Array` type.

- *Function parameters* are constant by default—this is different from Java rules.

- *Swift Functions* are of a reference type. Just as you can with a class type, you can pass functions as function parameters or return them as function return types. In practice, you would use closure expressions more frequently.

- *Closure expression* is one of the three types of **Closure** defined in Swift. It is an unnamed self-contained block of code that can be passed as a function parameter. The second type of closure is the global function mentioned right here, which is actually a special case of closure. The third type of closure is called a nested function declared inside a function, which is not used in this book.

Listing 2-17. Function Usages

```
func doWork(parm : String) -> String { // simple form
  return "TODO: " + parm
}
println(doWork("Swift"))

// External parameter names is part of the func signature
func doWork2(name parm : String) -> String {
// arg = arg.uppercaseString; // error: constant parm
  return "TODO: " + parm
}
```

```
println(doWork2(name: "Swift"))

// use # to indicate same name for internal and external
func doWork3(#name: String) -> String {
  return "TODO: " + name
}
println(doWork3(name: "Swift"))

// With default parm value, it also implies #, same external name
func doWork4(name: String = "Swift") -> String {
  return "TODO: " + name
}
println(doWork4()) // default parm value

// parm is constant by default unless declaring it with var
func doWork5(var name: String = "Swift") -> String {
  name = name.uppercaseString;
  return "TODO: " + name;
}

// variadic parms
func sumNumbers(parms : Int...) -> Int {
  var sum = 0
  for number in parms {
    sum += number
  }
  return sum
}
println(sumNumbers(2,5,8))

// func is a type, can be used for parm or return type.
func separateByAnd(p1: String, p2: String) -> String {
  return p1 + " and " + p2
}
func printTwoString(p1: String, p2: String, format: (String, String)->
String) {
  println(format(p1, p2))
}
printTwoString("Horse", "Carrot", separateByAnd)

// closure expression is unnamed func
printTwoString("Horse", "Carrot",
  {(p1: String, p2: String) -> String in
    return p1 + " and " + p2
  })
```

```
printTwoString("Horse", "Carrot",
  {p1, p2 in // type inferences
    return p1 + " and " + p2
  })
printTwoString("Horse", "Carrot",
  { // Inference and shorthanded parm names, $0, $1 ...
    return $0 + " and " + $1
  })
```

You may get by with not using most of the shorthand options at first, but for iOS programming, you definitely will need to get used to the external parameter names, because they are used heavily in iOS frameworks.

Class

Swift classes contain similar elements to Java classes. The simplest Java-like class form can be depicted as shown in Listing 2-18.

Listing 2-18. Simple Java-Like Swift Class

```
class SimpleClass {
  var mProperty : Int = 0 // public int mProperty ...
  var mConstant : String = "MyKey" // public String ...
  func myMethod(name: String) -> Void { println(name)}
}
```

Property

Java fields can be mapped to Swift properties as shown previously in Listing 2-18; they are called **stored properties**. In Swift, properties can do more than Java fields. Listing 2-19 demonstrates the following Swift property usages:

- *Stored property*: Java field.

- *Computed property*: For derived values.

- *Property observer*: Optional coding block that responds to changes in a property value.

- *Type property*: Similar to a Java class variable, but the stored type property is not supported in the Swift class type yet. Since struct type property is now supported, you may choose to define an inner struct for porting Java static variables as a workaround for now.

Listing 2-19. Swift Class Property

```
class MyClass {
  var width = 10, height = 10 // stored properties

  // computed properties, can have set as well
  var size : Int {
    get {
      return width * height
    }
  }

  var size2 : Int { // readonly, shorthanded
    return width * height
  }

  // property observer
  var depth : Int = 10 {
    willSet {
      println("depth (\(depth)) will be set to \(newValue)")
    }
    didSet {
      println("depth (\(depth)) was be set from \(oldValue)")
    }
  }

  // Swift class Type property,
  class var MyComputedTypeProperty : String {
    return "Only computed Type property is supported"
  }

  // use inner struct stored Type property as a workaround
  struct MyStatic {
    static let MyConst = "final static in Java"
    static var MyVar: String?
  }
}

println(MyClass.MyStatic.MyConst)
MyClass.MyStatic.MyVar = "class var in Java"
println(MyClass.MyStatic.MyVar)
```

Method

Methods are functions defined inside a type context (i.e., a class). They are still functions as described previously (see Listing 2-17). You can define instance methods or class methods just as Java does. Listing 2-20 shows the following typical method usages:

- Method declarations enforce external names implicitly, except for the first parameter. This is different from the global function (see the "Functions" section). All iOS Objective-C methods are ported to Swift using this convention.

- Use class func to declare class type methods, or static func to declare type methods in struct or enum types.

Listing 2-20. Common Method Usages

```
class MyClass {

///////// methods copied from Listing 2-17 //////////
  func doWork(parm : String) -> String { // just like func
    return "TODO: " + parm
  }

  // default parm value, always imply externl parm name
  func doWork2(name: String = "Swift") -> String {
    return "TODO: " + name
  }

  // func is a type, can be used for parm or return type, etc.
  func separateByAnd(p1: String, p2: String) -> String {
    return p1 + " and " + p2
  }

  func printTwoString(p1:String, p2:String, format:(String, String)->String)
{
    println(format(p1, p2))
  }

  // Type methods, aka Java class static method
  class func DoWork(parm : String) -> String {
    return "TODO: (Just like Java class static method)" + parm
  }
}
```

```
var c = MyClass()
println(c.doWork("Swift"))
println(c.doWork2()) // default parm value
println(c.doWork2(name: "Swift")) // external name enforced

// closure is unnamed func
c.printTwoString("Horse", p2: "Carrot", format: c.separateByAnd)
// Inference and shorthanded parm names apply to method, too.
c.printTwoString("Apple", p2: "Orange", format: {
  return $0 + " and " + $1
  })

MyClass.DoWork("Swift Type method")
```

Reference Type vs. Value Types

Just as in Java, reference types are passed by reference (the reference to the instance is copied to another variable) and values types are passed by copy (the whole value type instance is copied to another memory space). However, you do need to pay attention to certain differences:

- Similar to Java, your custom classes are reference types. Primitives, structs, and enums are value types.

- Unlike Java, some of the frequently used data types are value types, including String, Dictionary and Array (they are not classes in Swift). This is very nice, but may surprise you in the beginning.

- Since Dictionary and Array are value types, they are copied during assignment. The contained items are also deep-copied if they are value types.

- You will encounter the Swift NSString, NSArray, and NSDictionary because they are directly ported from counterpart Objective-C Foundation framework classes. They are all implemented as classes, and are thus reference types.

iOS Project Anatomy

Most GUI apps are composed of more than programming source code; for example, a typical iOS project contains Swift or Objective-C source code, libraries, storyboard files, images or multimedia non-code application resources, an application-information property Info.plist file, and so forth. Xcode compiles and builds the whole project and bundles all the artifacts required for an app into an archive file with an .app file extension, and signs the .app file with the appropriate signing certificate.

Let's translate a simple HelloMobile ADT project to Xcode so that you can visualize these software artifacts in a typical iOS app. The Android app in Figure 2-7 was created using the ADT **Create Android Project** template:

- It only has one screen: one Java Fragment class and one layout file.

- On this screen, it has an EditText to take user input. When the **Hello...** button is pressed, it shows a greeting on a TextView.

Figure 2-7. HelloMobile, Android version

To create the HelloMobile iOS app, start Xcode and proceed with the following steps:

1. Select **Create a new Xcode project** (See Figure 1-3) from the **Welcome to Xcode** launch screen. Or, you can select **File ➤ New ➤ Project...** from Xcode's top menu bar.

2. Select **iOS Application**, then choose **Single View Application** as the project template (see Figure 2-8).

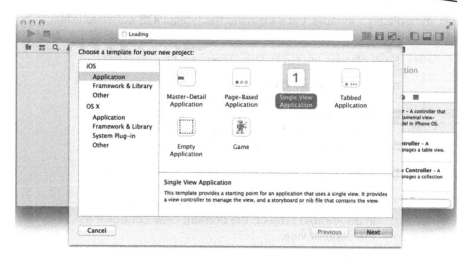

Figure 2-8. *Single View Application template*

3. Complete the following fields to finish the new-project creation:

    a. *Product Name*: HelloMobile

    b. *Organization Name*: for example, PdaChoice

    c. *Organization Identifier*: for example, com.liaollc

    d. Language: Swift

    e. Click the **Next** button when done.

    f. Select a folder to save your HelloMobile project.

The bare-bones HelloMobile iOS project is created and it now appears in the Xcode **Project Navigator** area (see Figure 2-9).

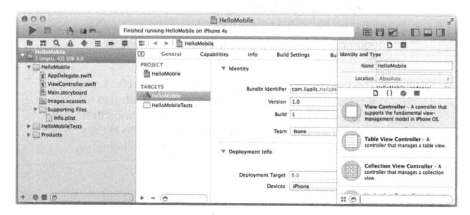

Figure 2-9. *HelloMobile project*

It is immediately runnable. Let's examine the typical iOS software artifacts in an Xcode project, which comprise the iOS app:

- Swift classes in `.swift` files. There are two classes:

    a. `AppDelegate.swift`: Each iOS app must have one `AppDelegate` class. Similar to `android.app.Application`, you don't need to modify this file if your program doesn't need to track the global application state.

    b. `ViewController.swift`: There is a `ViewController` class paired with the content view. The intended purpose is the same as the Android Fragment class in an Android project: the content view controller for the content view.

- `Main.storyboard` file with `.storyboard` file extension:

    a. You commonly create one storyboard scene per content view and use only one storyboard file for all content views so you can visually implement the linkages among them.

- `Images.xcassets`. This is where you put your image assets, in what is called the assets catalog:

    a. Developers should provide different assets for each device configuration. This is done for the same purpose as providing alternative resources in Android.

    b. PNG and JPEG image formats are both supported as of this writing. Using the assets catalog is not a must. You may drop any resource files into the Xcode project. (You may want to create a folder to organize them yourself.)

- `Info.plist` file. This file describes how the app is configured and the required capabilities the system needs to know:

    a. The best Android analogy is the `AndroidManifest.xml` file, but not exactly. You may glance through this file to get a feel for the configurations and settings that Xcode needs to know about the app. Xcode initially creates it in XML format, which you can edit directly.

- Unlike ADT projects that must follow the ADT project-folder structure, you can organize your project structure any way you want. For example, normally I manually create Java-package-like folders to organize my Swift classes and create a res folder to organize any resources files, including the Images.xcassets.

  a. In Xcode, the folder can be a actual folder of a light-blue color (e.g., the Images.xcassets folder).

  b. Folders in Xcode can also be just a tag, called a **group**, with a yellow color (e.g., HelloMobile, Supporting Files, etc.). Their actual location could be in any of the physical subfolders, but you should not care.

- Xcode 6 automatically creates a unit test target for your primary project. It contains a TestCase class skeleton in which you can write your unit test code. Although you will not use this feature in this book, it is actually very useful.

- **Project Settings** and **Target Settings** instruct Xcode how to compile and build the projects. To show the Project Settings, select the top-level application name in the Xcode **Project Navigator** area (see Figure 2-9). The Project Settings editor shows in the **Editor** area:

  a. For this simple project, you don't need to modify anything. But you should glance through the editor to get a quick idea of what Xcode requires to compile and build the executable.

The iOS app is not completed yet, but it has everything a typical iOS app should have.

Xcode Storyboard

ANDROID ANALOGY

There is no storyboard-like feature in ADT. You use the Graphic Layout Editor to create one content view in one layout file at a time.

Use the Xcode Storyboarding feature to visually compose the UI for your app. As its name implies, not only does it create individual screens and UI widgets, but it also lets you compose the whole app as one storyboard. Since iOS apps are all GUI apps, this tool will greatly determine your productivity in creating iOS apps through the following actions:

- Drag and drop **View Controller** from the **Object Library** to create a content view, called a Storyboard **Scene**.

- Drag and drop UI widgets from the **Object Library** onto the Storyboard **Scene** (content view), and position the widget appropriately.

- Implement Auto Layout to make the UI widgets and content view flexible and adaptive for various screen sizes, similar to the Android relative layout manager.

- Implement specific content views for specific **size classes** of different devices.

- Link the UI widgets to the properties of the view controller via **outlets**, and write code to respond to UI widget events.

- You can even draw the view controller transitions all within the storyboard editor.

There are other subviews in the **Utility** area that you can select from the top selector tool bar. All of them are important; you should take a moment to get familiar with them (see Figure 2-10):

- **File Inspector:** Shows you the actual file identity and document type options in Xcode.

- **Quick Help Inspector:** Shows you the reference doc.

- **Identity Inspector:** Shows you the Swift class from SDK or your custom class that is associated with the item in the storyboard.

- **Attributes Inspector:** This is our primary interest now. You will see different attributes for different widgets.

- **Size Inspector:** Shows you the rectangular area in which the widget is located.

- **Connections Inspector:** Lets you draw the connection to the view controller. I will discuss this later (see "Interact with Content View" in Chapter 3).

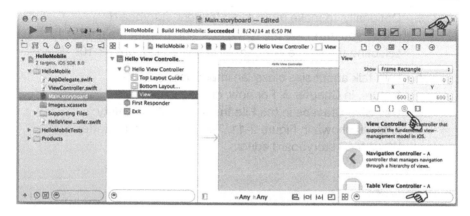

Figure 2-10. Select UI components from Object Library

Now is the time for you to get familiar with Xcode Storyboarding feature. The iOS HelloMobile project doesn't look like the counterpart Android app yet; it only has one screen in the Main.storyboard file, which is empty. The counterpart Android layout file has three UI widgets: EditText, TextView, and a hello Button.

First you will Implement the user interface of the HelloMobile iOS app. Xcode storyboard provides everything you need for this mission.

Object Library and Attributes Inspector

ANDROID ANALOGY

Drag and drop the UI widgets from Palette View in the ADT Graphical Layout Editor and set the widget attributes in the layout file.

You need to add three UI widgets to the content view, just as in the counterpart Android app, using the following steps:

1. Select the Main.storyboard file in the **Project Navigator**. Figure 2-10 depicts the storyboard editor in the **Editor** area. Currently, there is only one screen, known as a storyboard scene.

2. Select the **Object Library** from the Library selector bar in the **Utility** area. This is where you can find the UI widgets and elements to compose the storyboard.

3. Optionally, to make more room for your storyboard editor, you may hide the **Navigator** and **Debug** areas by selecting the toggle buttons, as indicated in Figure 2-10.

4. I will talk about size class, an important new iOS 8 feature, in Chapter 3. For now, disable it: uncheck **Use Size Classes** in the **File Inspector** of the **Utility** area, as shown in Figure 2-11. This will give you a better WYSIWYG storyboard editor.

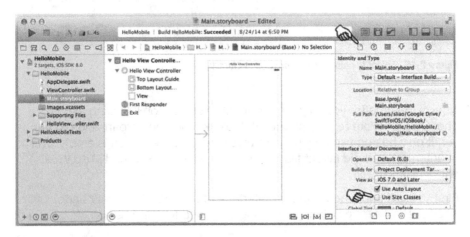

Figure 2-11. Disable Size Classes in File Inspector

5. To add the UI widget to storyboard scene, find the desired UI widget from **Object Library** and drag it to the existing View in the Storyboard scene. Both Android and iOS screens must have one root view, and any view element should be added to a parent view. This forms the parent-child view hierarchy.

    a. You must select the parent view (see pointer in Figure 2-11) first so you can drop the TextField element onto it.

    b. You may browse and select the UI widgets from **Object Library**. The list is long, so the search bar on the bottom is very useful for finding the right widget. Type the name of the iOS widget, as shown in Figure 2-10, or just type in your best guess as many characters as needed.

> **Tip** The iOS widgets you need are called `TextField`, `Label`, and `Button`.

    c. To position the newly added `TextField`, drag it to where you want it to be. Xcode gives you guide lines to show you when the widgets are at certain positions of the common interests, such as in the center, or aligned to any other widgets (see Figure 2-12).

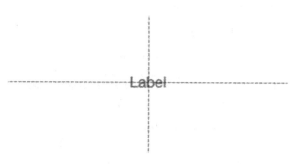

Figure 2-12. *Guide lines*

    d. Figure 2-13 shows the three simple UI widgets added to the storyboard scene.

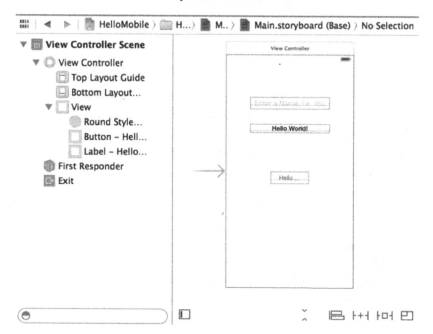

Figure 2-13. *Three simple UI widgets*

6. Just as in Android, the attributes of UI widgets in Swift affect the look, feel, and behavior of the widgets, and you can change them visually. You can find and modify these attributes in the **Attributes Inspector** located in the **Utility** area. To make the TextField like the Android counterpart, modify the following attributes:

    a. Font size: System 24

    b. Placeholder (a.k.a. android:hint): "Enter a Name, e.g., You"

    c. Alignment: center

    d. TextField has a handful of attributes. Glance through them and you should have no problem relating them to the counterpart attributes you normally use in Android EditText.

    e. Switch to **Size Inspector** view and change the width to 200. You will need to drag the TextField to reposition it to center horizontally.

7. To make the Label widget like the Android counterpart TextView, modify the following attributes:

    a. Text: for example, "Hello World!"

    b. Font: for example, System 20 or Headline

    c. Alignment: center

    d. Lines: 1

    e. Switch to the **Size Inspector** and change the width to 200. You will need to drag the label to reposition it to center horizontally.

8. To make the Button widget like the Android counterpart, modify the following attributes:

    a. Text: "Hello World!"

    b. Title: "Hello ..."

9. To preview your storyboard in Xcode, select the **Assistant Editor** button on the toolbar and select **Preview** in the Assistant Editor, as shown in Figure 2-14.

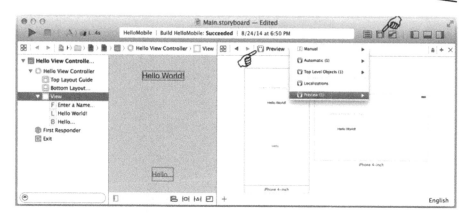

Figure 2-14. Three simple widgets added to storyboard

The look and feel in portrait mode is close enough for our purposes: using a storyboard to visually compose the content view without writing a single line of code. The iOS HelloMobile is not completed yet: the Hello ... button doesn't read "Hello...", and the landscape mode is not acceptable yet. Both are important topics and have their own sections in Chapter 3.

In this exercise, I just wanted to give you a quick look of the Xcode storyboard editor. The Xcode workspace seems quite different from Eclipse. Spend a moment to get familiar with the Xcode workspace, including the storyboard editor, the **Utility** area, selector tool bar, and so forth. Xcode storyboarding is a very important tool that will greatly influence your productivity when creating iOS apps.

Summary

On the surface, you actually learned about a lot of things in this chapter. You started with a discussion of Swift–Java language comparisons to learn their similarities, then you went over Swift language topics to highlight the new language features. However, the rest of the book will focus on iOS programming instead of the Swift language. The code will address readability as opposed to being concise using new tricks. You surely won't have a problem reading all the Swift code in the rest of the book. Sooner or later, though, you will need the reference document to the Swift programming language, which is available free in iTunes (https://itunes. apple.com/us/book/swift-programming-language/id881256329).

You created a HelloMobile iOS project using Xcode to visualize a typical iOS application structure so you can visualize. You also got your first taste of the Xcode storyboard, which is very important and which you will use for every iOS app, including all the sample projects in this book—so plan on revisiting the storyboard repeatedly.

A Roadmap for Porting

In Part II, you will plan and structure your iOS apps following the iOS thinking process, which can be explained in Android vocabulary using the common top-down design approach. After you finish Part II, you will be able to create simple but meaningful iOS apps with rich UI components, and to handle common CRUD operations locally and remotely.

Your migrating-to-Swift roadmap follows the common top-down approach, with translation guidelines in lower-level implementation using your comfortable Android vocabulary, which you can then relate to the mobile functions that you normally do in Android.

Part II shows you the common screen-navigation patterns that you normally encounter in your Android apps, and how to carry out the same tasks in iOS apps. Not only do you get a high-level runnable iOS storyboard; you also get Android-like MVC structured classes that are mapped to the counterpart Swift classes. The rest of Part II provides instructions on how to convert the common mobile implementation tasks from Android SDK to iOS SDK— including UI, saving data, networking, and so forth—that are widely used in almost any Android GUI app. Again, after completing Part II, you will be capable of creating iOS apps that are simple but meaningful.

Chapter 3

Structure Your App

To implement your software, you will make design decisions based on how you'd like to structure your app in terms of organizing your code into classes. To decide your iOS app structure up front, the top-down approach and model-view-controller (MVC) design pattern are recommended and actually embedded in the iOS SDK and tools. MVC is also implicitly embedded in Android SDK (with different vocabularies), and if you are used to the top-down approach for creating your Android apps, where you design the application workflow prior to detailing each individual screen, it is even easier for you to switch your programming thinking process between iOS and Android.

In this first step, you are aiming at class-level mapping from the Android counterparts. I will discuss MVC first, followed by how to create the iOS storyboard in Xcode. With the guided screen navigation patterns, your iOS storyboard naturally breaks your iOS apps into MVC components that can be mapped from their Android counterparts.

Model-View-Controller

ANDROID ANALOGY

- **Content view**: Layout files
- **Content view controller**: Fragment class
- **Delegate**: Java event listener
- **Container view controller**: the Activity class that coordinates the child Fragments in it

MVC immediately breaks the GUI app into three layers. The iOS MVC design pattern specifies that a GUI application consists of a data **model**, a presentation **view**, and **controller** layers, as shown in Figure 3-1.

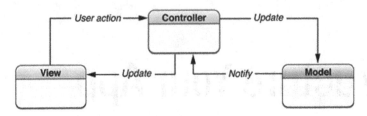

Figure 3-1. The iOS MVC design pattern

Although there seem to be no explicit MVC vocabularies defined in the Android SDK, it implicitly enforces separating content view from the content view controller in terms of Layout files and Fragment classes.

In iOS, you explicitly use the MVC vocabularies: content view and content view controller. You naturally break down your iOS app into MVC classes, starting with creating a storyboard prototype using the Xcode storyboard editor.

Unless your app only has one screen, you need to decide how to implement navigations and screen transitions among multiple view controllers. You need an optional MVC participant: Container View Controller. In Android, there seems to be no explicit framework class that does the work for you. However, the parent-child relationship between Activity and Fragment makes the parent Activity a natural candidate for the Container View Controller participant. In practice, I use the parent Activity to manage the child Fragments, including for navigation code.

In iOS, the SDK provides several Container View Controllers for screen navigation; you simply choose the appropriate Container View Controller class and let the iOS framework facilitate the tasks for you.

I'll start with content view and content view controller, then talk about the Container View Controller next.

Content View

ANDROID ANALOGY

Android Layout file.

A content view provides a visible area so that users can interact with the app. The content view defines how to render itself with contents and can interact with user actions. To create content views in iOS, use Xcode **storyboard**.

Recall that in the iOS HelloMobile app, you drew the UI widgets in the storyboard scene in a very similar fashion to what you normally do in ADT: drag and drop the widgets to draw them on the parent view. However, this iOS content view is not adaptive to other device types and screen orientations yet. You can easily observe the landscape problem in the **Assistant Editor** previews (see Figure 2-14). Creating adaptive content views for various screen sizes is a common task in both iOS and Android. In Android, you achieve this via alternative layout resources and layout managers. In iOS, you essentially use iOS platform features for the same purposes:

- *Auto Layout*: This works best with responsive UX designs that are agnostic/adaptive to screens sizes.

- *Size classes*: These provide ultimate flexibility for customizing the screens for different screen sizes.

Auto Layout

ANDROID ANALOGY

RelativeLayout.

You can think of iOS Auto Layout as Android RelativeLayout: you position each UI widget by aligning or spacing it relative to neighbors or the parent view.

The three widgets in the current iOS HelloMobile project are not positioned properly in landscape mode (see Figure 2-14). Use iOS Auto Layout to fix this while learning its uses.

While extremely powerful, some Xcode editors or operations are collapsed in the menus and could be difficult to locate for a beginner. Figure 3-2 depicts some quick tips:

- If you cannot find any editor or navigator, go to **View ➤ ...** in the Xcode top menu bar.

- Auto Layout operations are grouped in **Editor ➤ ...** in the Xcode top menu bar.

- There are four small buttons in the bottom toolbar of the storyboard editor. They offer quick Auto Layout operations and give you some visual hints of what they are.

- **Assistant Editor** that you will use next.

- The view selector in the **Utility** area allows you to switch between several inspectors. You will use them a lot in the next chapter, too.

Figure 3-2. Storyboard Auto Layout operations in Xcode

Continue working on the HelloMobile project. Do the following:

1. Storyboard **Preview** in **Assistant Editor** is extremely useful for immediately seeing any changes for the selected storyboard scene:

   a. Select the main.storyboard file and open **Assistant Editor** (see the right pointer in Figure 3-3).

   b. Click the **Assistant** menu button to select Preview (see the left pointer in Figure 3-3).

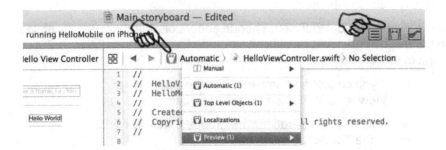

Figure 3-3. Two steps to reach the Xcode storyboard Preview

2. **Horizontal Center** the `TextField` **in Container** to create an x-alignment constraint as shown in Figure 3-4:

   a. Select the `TextField` in the storyboard editor.

   b. In the Xcode top menu bar, select **Editor** ➤ **Align** ➤ **Horizontal Center in Container**.

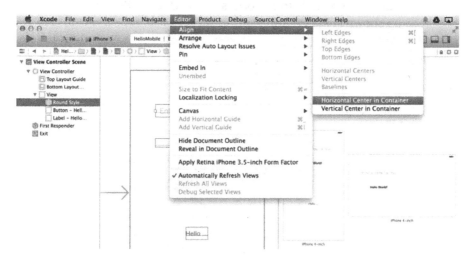

Figure 3-4. *Using **Horizontal Center in Container** on the* `TextField` *in Auto Layout editor*

3. Use **Vertical Center in Container** to create a y-alignment constraint (see Figure 3-5):

   a. From the Xcode top menu bar, select **Editor** ➤ **Align** ➤ **Vertical Center in Container**.

   b. In the **Attributes Inspector** in the **Utility** area, to position the `TextField` at the one-sixth of the view height instead of half, you can apply a **Multiplier** of 3.

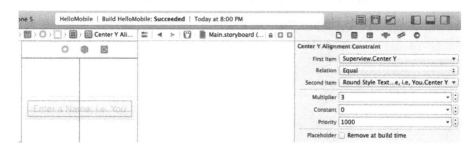

Figure 3-5. *Creating constraint y-alignment constraint using a multiplier*

> **Note**   Use Multiplier or Constant to offset the second item position:
>
> (first item center position) == (second item center) * multiplier + constant

4. Select **Resolve Auto Layout issue ➤ Update Frames** as shown in Figure 3-6.

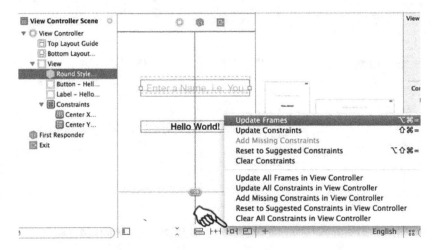

*Figure 3-6. Using **Update Frames** to reposition the UI widgets based on constraints*

5. Select the **Hello World!** label and click the **Pin** button to add multiple constraints for appropriate spacing and widgets height as shown in Figure 3-7:

    a. Pin the **Top** space to the nearest widget, the TextField, with 48.5 pixels.

    b. Pin both **Leading** and **Trailing** spaces to the nearest widget, its parent View, with 60 pixels.

    c. Pin its **Height** to be 21 pixels.

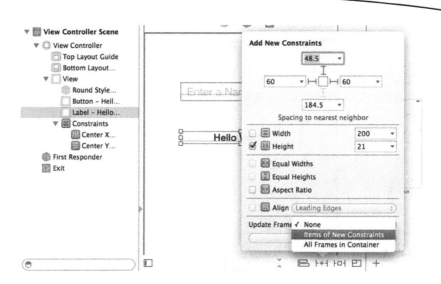

Figure 3-7. Spacing Hello World! label relative to its neighbors

> **Note** The combined constraints need to make sense without ambiguity. You can set priority to each individual constraint. However, if you start using priority to resolve conflicts, you might want to think about using fewer constraints for your purpose.

6. Select the Hello... button. You can align it similar to the TextField:

    a. Use **Horizontal Center in Container** to create an x-alignment constraint.

    b. Use **Vertical Center in Container** to create a y-alignment constraint with **Multiplier** to be 0.75.

Using the Auto Layout with responsive UX designs immediately provides proper landscape layout. Figure 3-8 shows the previews in both landscape and portrait modes for iPhone 4-inch and 3.5-inch modes. Click the + icon (see the pointer in Figure 3-8) to add multiple previews for different devices.

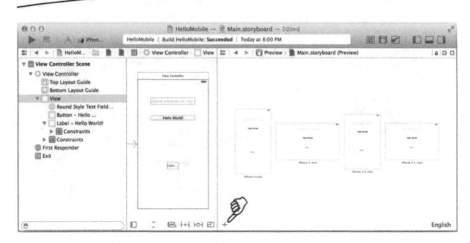

Figure 3-8. Auto Layout with responsive UX design

Size Classes

```
ANDROID ANALOGY
```

Provide alternative layout resources for different screen sizes.

While Auto Layout provides an effective way to implement responsive UX for various screen sizes, it may not utilize the valuable mobile-screen real estate in the most efficient ways. For example, it is fairly common to portray landscape view different from portrait due to different aspect ratios, or to have tablet-specific UX design, and so forth.

Prior to iOS 8, you generally implemented two storyboards, one for iPhone and one for iPad. The concept is very similar to Android alternative-layout resources for different screen sizes. Beginning with iOS 8, **Size Classes** were introduced to solve this common programming issue by using the abstract presentations of device sizes in terms of horizontal widths and vertical heights. The current iOS devices can be classified as shown in Table 3-1.

Table 3-1. iOS Device Size Classes

Size Classes	Compact Width • iPhone portrait width • iPhone landscape width	Regular Width • iPad portrait width • iPad landscape width
Compact Height: • iPhone landscape height	iPhone in landscape	Customized view controller
Regular Height: • iPad portrait height • iPad landscape height • iPhone portrait height	iPhone in portrait	iPad in portrait iPad in landscape

You can provide all the implementation for all size classes all in one storyboard!

Recall the iOS `HelloMobile` app—it only works in iPhone portrait mode (see Figure 2-14) and it disabled the Size Classes feature. Now you should enable Size classes to demonstrate its use. Do the following:

1. As shown in Figure 3-9, enable the **Use Size Classes** (bottom pointer) in the **File Inspector** (accessed as shown by the top two pointers).

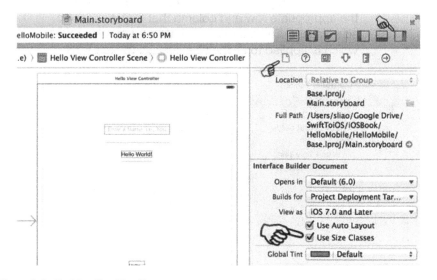

Figure 3-9. Enabling Use Size Classes

2. Use **Assistant Editor** to preview iPhone and iPad screens. Size Classes could be overwhelming in the beginning, but I found the previews very helpful (see Figure 3-10).

    a. The scenes are converted to the most adaptive size class: (wAny hAny). The Auto Layout constraints are also preserved in this size class. You immediately get the iPad scene working as expected.

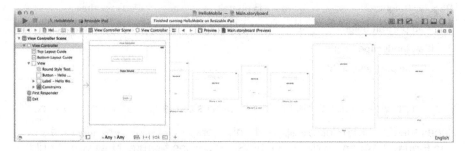

Figure 3-10. Size Classes preview

3. Click the **Size Class** control to select the size class (see Figure 3-11).

    a. Hover your mouse to see the highlight and title changes. Comparing with Table 3-1, you can select the appropriate row and column that targets specific size classes. The default is **Any Width | Any Height**, which is applied to all the size classes to start with.

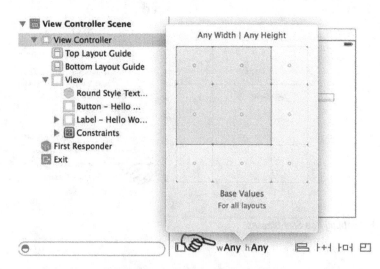

Figure 3-11. Using the size class selector to select a specific size class

4. To provide a specific layout for an iPhone landscape scene, select the **Compact Width | Compact Height** as shown in Figure 3-12.

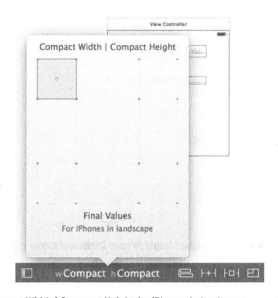

Figure 3-12. Compact Width I Compact Height for iPhones in landscape

5. To demonstrate the powerful Size Class feature, start fresh for the compact-compact size class. From the top menu bar, select **Clear Constraints in View Controller** from **Editor ➤ Resolve Auto Layout Issues**. This only clears the Auto Layout constraints in the selected size class; you can see the constraints still there but grayed out.

6. Drag the widgets to reposition them, just to get a quick idea—you don't need to be precise (see Figure 3-13).

    a. Since you are providing a custom layout explicitly for iPhones in landscape, you actually can draw the positions precisely and let storyboard do the rest by choosing **Reset to Suggested Constraints in View Controller** in the top menu bar from **Editor ➤ Resolve Auto Layout Issues**.

    b. If you tried the preceding step, select **Clear Constraints in View Controller** again to have a clean start for creating Auto Layout constraints.

Figure 3-13. Two-sided view for compact height (iPhone landscape mode)

7. For the TextField, add the following Auto Layout constraints:

    a. Use **Horizontal Center in Container** to create an x-alignment constraint with **Multiplier, 2**.

    b. Use **Vertical Center in Container** to create a y-alignment constraint with **Multiplier, 1.5**.

    c. From the top menu bar, select Update Frame at **Editor ➤ Resolve Auto Layout Issues**.

    d. To update the existing constraints, either select the constraint from the storyboard navigator, or select the widget on the scene first to see and click on the guided line in the storyboard scene. Use **Attributes Inspector** in the **Utility** area (see Figure 3-14) to update any constraint attribute.

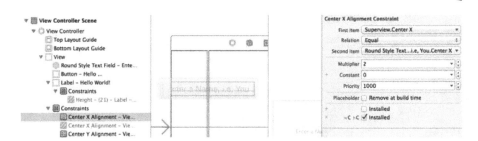

Figure 3-14. *Updating the Auto Layout constraint*

8. For the `Label`, add the following Auto Layout constraints
    in the same way as in step 7:

    a. Use **Horizontal Center in Container** to create an
        x-alignment constraint with **Multiplier, 2**.

    b. Use **Vertical Center in Container** to create a
        y-alignment constraint with **Multiplier, 0.75**.

    c. From the top menu bar, select **Update Frame** at
        Editor ➤ Resolve Auto Layout Issues.

9. For the `Button`, add the following Auto Layout
    constraints in the same way as in step 7:

    a. Use **Horizontal Center in Container** to create an
        x-alignment constraint with **Multiplier, 0.67**.

    b. Use **Vertical Center in Container** to create a
        y-alignment constraint with **Multiplier, 1**.

    c. From the top menu bar, select **Update Frame** at
        Editor ➤ Resolve Auto Layout Issues.

All the device classes in previews look good as expected (Figure 3-15).

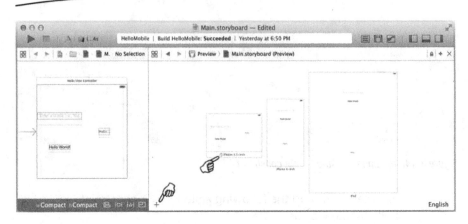

Figure 3-15. Device classes previewed in the storyboard editor

You can run the app in all emulators to see the work in action. The iPhone 4s emulator is shown in Figure 3-16.

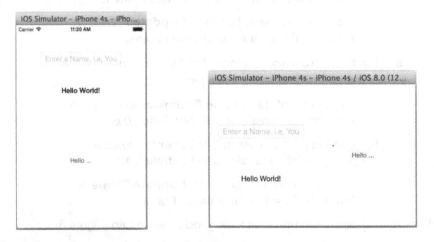

Figure 3-16. iPhone4s portrait and landscape size class

Content View Controller

ANDROID ANALOGY

Fragment.

The Content View Controller participant pairs with a content view (see **Figure 3-1**). In both the iOS and Android programming paradigms, the content view normally is created statically (i.e., by layout.xml or storyboard). The Content View Controller class manages the content view to present the dynamic behavior of the user interface by conveying information to and interacting with users. You normally subclass Fragment to create your Content View Controllers in Android. In iOS, you create a class subclassing from UIViewController for the same purpose.

Your primary Content View Controller tasks are:

- Pair with its own content view

- Keep object references to the UI widgets in content view

- Implement methods to respond to widget events.

In iOS, you normally use the storyboard editor to connect the UI widgets or events to your code to facilitate these common programming tasks.

Pair with Content View

ANDROID ANALOGY

Inflate the layout.xml file in Fragment.onCreateView(...).

In iOS, you normally create a storyboard for your apps first (like the iOS HelloMobile project). Generally, for every storyboard scene (content view), you create a Swift class subclassed from UIViewController to pair with it.

The iOS HelloMobile project is not completed yet: it only renders the initial screen but does not do anything when you click on the Hello... button. You need a functional Content View Controller that can fulfill this responsibility. The **Single View Application** Template pairs a controller class for you already: ViewController.swift. To demonstrate the whole subject, don't use this class; instead, do the following to create our own class:

1. Create a new file for a new Swift class:

    a. Right-click on the HelloMobile folder in the **Navigator** area, then select **New File ... ➤ iOS ➤ Source ➤ Swift File** (see Figure 2-3).

    b. Save the file as HelloViewController.swift.

    c. Create the HelloViewController class subclassed from UIViewController as shown in Listing 3-1.

Listing 3-1. HelloViewController Class Skeleton

```
import UIKit
class HelloViewController: UIViewController {
  // TODO
}
```

2. Pair the storyboard scene with the HelloViewController class (see Figure 3-17):

   a. Select Main.storyboard to open the storyboard editor.

   b. Select the view controller in the storyboard scene and open the **Identity Inspector** in the **Utility** area.

   c. Enter HelloViewController in the **Custom Class** field to pair the storyboard scene with the HelloViewController class.

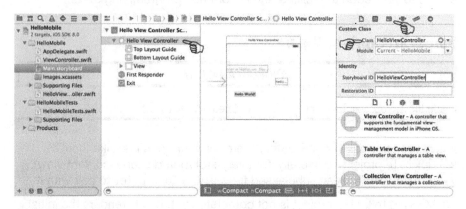

Figure 3-17. Identity Inspector to pair with view controller

Specifying the custom class in **Identity Inspector** is all you need to pair with the content view controller.

Interact with Content View

ANDROID ANALOGY

In the Fragment view controller class,

rootView.findViewById(...) to get the object reference.

Register event listener using the setOnXxxListener(...) methods.

Generally in both Android and iOS, you create UI widgets in a content view and your content view controller code updates the widget's states or interacts with users at runtime. In iOS, you use **Connections Inspector** to create IBOutlet and IBAction to facilitate this common programming task by drawing connections to your code in the Swift class:

■ IBOutlet: the view controller property that is connect to the widgets in the storyboard scene.

■ IBAction: the view controller method that is called when the widget events occur.

The following walks you through the steps to connect the UI widgets and delegates action events to your controller class:

1. Select Main.storyboard to open the storyboard editor.

   a. Open the storyboard **Assistant Editor**. The HelloViewController class should automatically open in the assistant editor.

   b. Sometimes the right file may not be opened automatically in the **Assistant Editor**, so you may need to select the right file manually (see Figure 3-18).

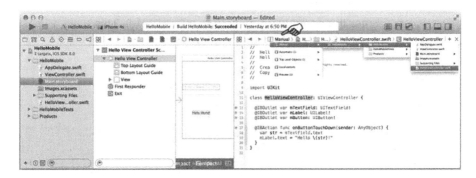

Figure 3-18. Selecting a file manually in Assistant Editor

2. Select the TextField in the storyboard scene (the left pointer in Figure 3-19), and open the **Connections Inspector** (the right pointer in Figure 3-19) as shown in Figure 3-19 (make sure the **Utility** Area is unfolded).

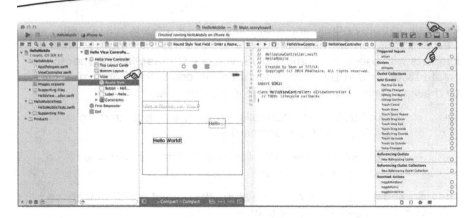

*Figure 3-19. Opening the **Connections Inspector***

3.   Create an IBOutlet for the TextField in the storyboard scene (see Figure 3-20).

   a.   Drag the circle next to **New Referencing Outlet** with three fingers (or hold the left trackpad button at the same time) and drop it inside the class. You should see the line from the circle as shown in Figure 3-20.

   b.   Enter the connection name (i.e., mTextField). This creates a property in the Swift class.

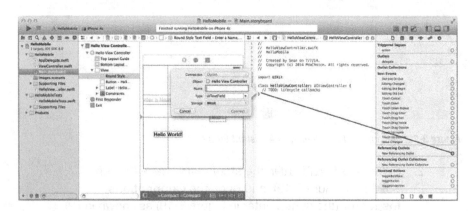

*Figure 3-20. IBOutlet in **Connections Inspector***

4.   Repeat steps 2 and 3 to create mLabel and mButton IBOutlets.

5. Create an `IBAction` for the button touch down events.

    a. Drag the circle next to **Touch Down** in **Sent Events** section and drop it inside the Swift class (see Figure 3-21).

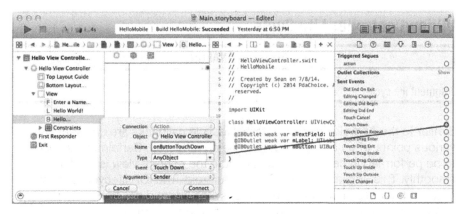

Figure 3-21. Creating an IBAction in the Connections Inspector

b. Enter the method name: i.e., `onButtonTouchDown`. This creates a method stub in the Swift class.

c. Add the Say-Hello code to complete the `IBAction` method implementation in `HelloViewController.swift` as shown in Listing 3-2.

Listing 3-2. HelloViewController with IBOutlet and IBAction

```swift
import UIKit

class HelloViewController: UIViewController {

  @IBOutlet weak var mTextField: UITextField!
  @IBOutlet weak var mLabel: UILabel!
  @IBOutlet weak var mButton: UIButton!

  @IBAction func onButtonTouchDown(sender: AnyObject) {
    var str = mTextField.text
    mLabel.text = "Hello \(str)!"
  }
}
```

This completes the whole HelloMobile iOS app. You can run the project in all iOS simulators to see the code in action.

You're almost done with the MVC topics. Just one more small lecture before we get into more fun stuff: UIViewController lifecycle events.

UIViewController Life Cycle

```
ANDROID ANALOGY
```

Fragment life cycle.

Similar to the Android Fragment class, lifecycle callbacks are called at various points when a content view is being rendered. Certain tasks need to be performed in certain states to ensure the content view is rendered smoothly. This applies to both iOS and Android. The iOS lifecycle concept may not be a beginner topic, but it is easy for Android developers to pick up because the purpose is the same: they want to perform certain computing tasks at the right time, with which Android developers are already familiar.

In Android, the lifecycle events are described as the states of the view controller itself. In iOS, these lifecycle events are directly related to the content view events, so you actually can visualize the effects better because they are directly related to the view-rendering process.

Implementing these view events is essentially the same as writing your Fragment lifecycle callback methods: you can choose to override these inherited system methods to receive timely callbacks if you wish.

viewDidLoad

```
ANDROID ANALOGY
```

Fragment.onCreate() and onCreateView().

iOS system calls the viewDidLoad() method when the view controller loads its content view from the storyboard scene. You commonly put the initialization code here.

viewWillAppear

```
                      ANDROID ANALOGY
```

onStart().

iOS system calls the viewWillAppear() method when the view is about to appear. Generally, you can safely translate the Android onStart() into this method.

viewDidAppear

```
                      ANDROID ANALOGY
```

onResume().

iOS system calls the viewDidAppear() method when the view becomes visible. Generally, you can safely translate the Android onResume() into this method.

viewWillDisappear

```
                      ANDROID ANALOGY
```

onPause().

The system calls the viewWillDisappear() method when the content view is about to become invisible—for example, leaving for another storyboard scene. This is usually where you should commit any changes that should be persisted beyond the current user session (because the user might not come back).

viewDidDisappear()

```
                      ANDROID ANALOGY
```

onStop().

The system calls the viewDidDisappear() method when the content view is not visible.

When implementing these lifecycle events, you almost always will want to call the corresponding super.viewXXX(), just like Android.

Screen Navigation Patterns

You commonly use multiple screens to convey hierarchical information to and interact with users. Considering the relatively small mobile screens, it is even more crucial that you use well-known navigation patterns to make mobile apps more predictable. A consistent and predictable navigation pattern guides users to complete a task with multiple screens. Efficient navigation is one of the cornerstones of a well-designed app.

This section will focus on the most common screen navigation patterns supported in both iOS and Android.

Storyboard Segue

Segue, pronounced "seg-way", is a type of a connection in storyboard that specifies transitions from one scene to another. For instance, you can create an Action Segue that is performed immediately when the action is triggered. More frequently, you will create a Manual Segue in storyboard and write logics to perform the segue. Depending on its transition type, the segue may require a Container View Controller. For example, to implement the typical navigation stack transitions, you will need a Navigation Controller in iOS.

The following steps will walk you through the steps of a storyboard segue:

1. Create a new Xcode project using **Single View Application** with a product name of Segues. (See Chapter 2, "iOS Project Anatomy" for step-by-step instructions)

2. Open Main.storyboard in the storyboard editor. It should look like Figure 3-22 when done.

   a. Add two Button widgets to the existing scene: one for Action Segue and the other for Manual Segue.

   b. Drop two ViewControllers onto the storyboard from **Object Library** to add two storyboard scenes. Add a UILabel to each scene with titles **"From Action Segue"** and **"From Manual Segue,"** respectively.

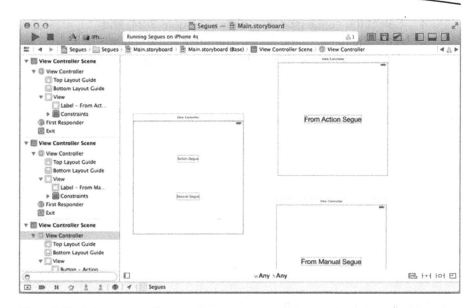

Figure 3-22. Segues preparation

3. Create an Action Segue from the Action Segue Button
    to the **From Action Segue** scene.

    a. Select the Action Segue Button and open the
        Connections Inspector in the **Utility** area.

    b. Drag the action outlet in the **Triggered Segue**
        section to **From Action Segue** view controller as
        shown in Figure 3-23.

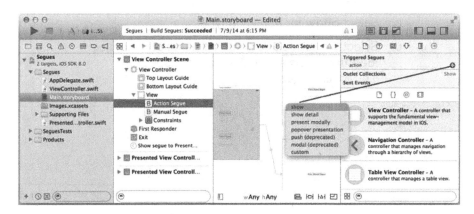

Figure 3-23. Creating an Action Segue

    c. Select **Show** for transition type.

4. Select the segue (see the pointer in Figure 3-24) and enter the name of the segue **Identifier** in the segue **Attributes Inspector** (i.e., actionSegue), as shown in Figure 3-24.

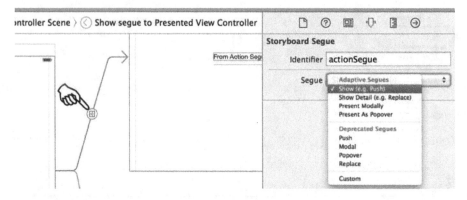

Figure 3-24. Selecting the segue and setting up the attributes

5. Create a Manual Segue from the presenting controller to the **From Manual Segue** view controller as shown in Figure 3-25:

   a. Select the presenting View Controller and open the **Connections Inspector** in the **Utility** area.

   b. Drag the circle (outlet) in the **Manual Triggered Segue** section to the **From Manual Segue** view controller.

   c. Select **Show** for transition type.

   d. Select the segue and enter the name of the segue **Identifier** in the segue **Attributes Inspector** (i.e., manualSegue).

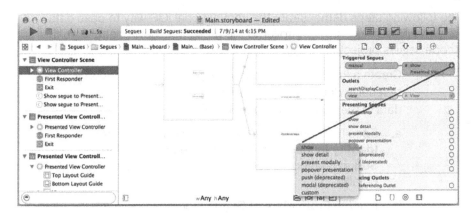

Figure 3-25. Creating a Manual Segue

6. Set up Manual Segue to be performed programmatically when the Manual Segue button is selected:

    a. Create an IBAction to ViewController class with the name onManualSegueTouchDown.

    b. In the onManualSegueTouchDown(...) method, use the code in Listing 3-3 to perform the manual segue.

Listing 3-3. Performing the Manual Segue

```
import UIKit
class ViewController: UIViewController {
  @IBAction func onManualSegueTouchDown(sender: AnyObject) {
    self.performSegueWithIdentifier("manualSegue", sender: sender)
  }
}
```

Run the app in different emulators to see these segues work in different size classes. Since iOS 8, the segues are presented in an adaptive manner to the size classes.

Pass Data with a Segue

The storyboard segues perform screen transitions nice and easy by drawing the segue connections. You don't even need a line of code for an Action Segue. However, you normally will need to pass data from the presenting view controller to the presented view controller, which cannot be done alone by the storyboard segue itself.

The following steps demonstrate the conventional iOS way to pass data from the presenting view controller to the presented view controller in the Xcode Segues project:

1. Create a PresentedViewController class with a property to receive data. Listing 3-4 simply prints the received data in the viewDidLoad() method.

    a. Specify the PresentedViewController class in the **Identity Inspector** to pair with the **From Action Segue** storyboard scene (see Figure 3-17 for details).

    b. Pair the **From Manual Segue** storyboard scene with the PresentedViewController class as well.

    c. Add a property, data, to receive the data from the presenting view controller.

Listing 3-4. Data Property to Receive Data from Presenting View Controller

```
import UIKit
class PresentedViewController: UIViewController {
  var data: String?
  override func viewDidLoad() {
    if let tmp = data {
      println("received data: \(tmp)")
    }
  }
  ...
}
```

2. The system invokes a prepareForSegue(...) method in the source view controller. You need to implement this method to receive the callback. To pass data from the source view controller, ViewController, override the prepareForSegue method as shown in Listing 3-5.

Listing 3-5. Presenting View Controller Override prepareForSegue

```
override func prepareForSegue(segue: UIStoryboardSegue, sender: AnyObject?)
{
  var identifier = segue.identifier
  var destVc = (segue.destinationViewController as PresentedViewController)
  destVc.data = "some data from presenting vc \(identifier)"
}
```

Container View Controller

ANDROID ANALOGY

Activity is the parent of child Fragments.

In iOS, screen navigations are primarily implemented by storyboard segues and the Container View Controller classes from SDK that facilitate the screen navigations. You may create subclasses from these system container view controllers, but normally you can just use them as is.

Navigation Stack

ANDROID ANALOGY

FragmentManager back stack.

The **Navigation Stack** is widely used to manage screen transitions, and particularly for displaying information hierarchy, such as a master drilldown list. To show the next screen, push the next view controller into the navigation stack. To go back to the previous screen, pop out the previous view controller in the navigation stack.

Create an iOS version of the following simple Android app that has an action bar, as shown in Figure 3-26. This simple Android app does the following:

- It has three content views.
- It uses FragmentManager API to create fragment transaction for screen transitions.
- The device back button automatically removes the FragmentTransaction from back stack.
- You probably used the Fragment Animation API to implement the slide-in and slide-out animations.

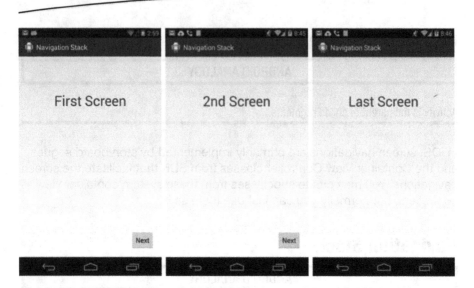

Figure 3-26. The Android NavigationStack app with three screens

In iOS, you draw appropriate storyboard segues with the UINavigationController Container View Controller to accomplish this navigation stack pattern. Let's create a new Xcode project to demonstrate the iOS way.

1. Create a new Xcode project using iOS **Single View Application** template (see chapter 2, "iOS Project Anatomy"). Name it NavigationStack.

2. Select Main.storyboard to open the storyboard in the **Editor** area. It has one scene already.

3. Add two more content view (scenes): drag ViewController from **Object Library** onto the storyboard twice. Figure 3-27 depicts the storyboard containing three scenes.

Figure 3-27. Three storyboard scenes in the NavigationStack project

4. Use the counterpart Android Screen One layout to guide you as you update the first storyboard scene:

a. Add a Label from the **Object Library**. Change its font size to **30** and text to "Screen One", and center its alignment with the **Attributes Inspector** in the **Utility** area.

b. Add Auto Layout constraints to center the label as shown in Figure 3-28.

Figure 3-28. Screen One label with center constraints

c. Add the Next button with the right and bottom space constraints to anchor the position as shown in Figure 3-29.

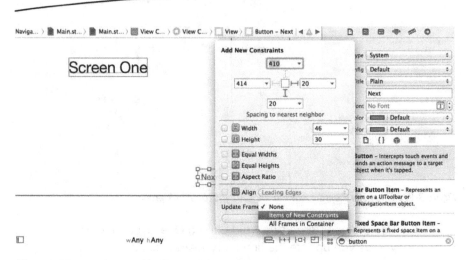

Figure 3-29. *Next button with alignment constraints*

5. Repeat step 4 to add a **"Screen Two"** Label and the
    Next button to the **Screen Two** scene.

6. Repeat step 4 to add a **"Screen Three"** Label to the
    Screen Three scene. Figure 3-30 shows the UI widgets
    added to storyboard.

Figure 3-30. *Three scenes with widgets in NavigationStack project*

7. Create an Action Segue from the Next button in Screen
    One to the Screen Two scene, and another Action
    Segue from the Next button in Screen Two to the Screen
    Three scene.

Figure 3-31 shows the results of the storyboard. Run the app to see what is
working and what is not working yet. Nothing is new yet, just repeated steps
that create storyboard scenes, UI widgets, Auto Layout constraints, and
segues that connect them together.

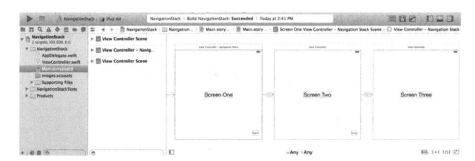

Figure 3-31. NavigationStack storyboard

UINavigationController

ANDROID ANALOGY

FragmentTransaction Back Stack

The only missing piece in this iOS project is a way to show the appropriate child view controller in the typical push and pop fashions. In iOS, the UINavigationController manages the push and pop screen navigation stack behaviors. It also provides a navigation bar that has a default back button, a title in the center, and an optional right button (see Figure 3-32).

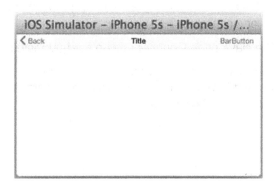

Figure 3-32. The UINavigationController navigation bar

All you need to do is to set up a UINavigationController that associates its root view controller with the first scene:

- Add a Navigation Controller from **Object Library**.
- Connect the root view controller segue (in **Connections Inspector**) to the first view controller.

You can accomplish both in one simple storyboard operation: embed the Screen One view controller in a Navigation Controller as shown in the following steps:

1. Select Screen One View Controller from the storyboard.

2. In the Xcode menu bar, select **Editor ➤ Embed In ➤ Navigation Controller** as shown in Figure 3-33.

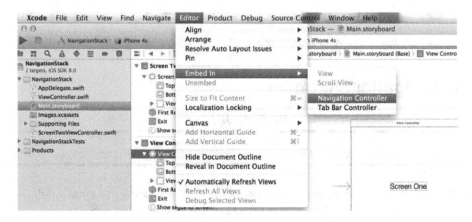

Figure 3-33. Creating a Navigation Controller

3. This creates a Navigation Controller and connects the root view controller segue to the Screen One view controller (see Figure 3-34).

    a. The Navigation Controller has a `NavigationBar`.

    b. The root view controller automatically gets a `NavigationItem` where you can add a center `title` and a `rightBarButtonItem`.

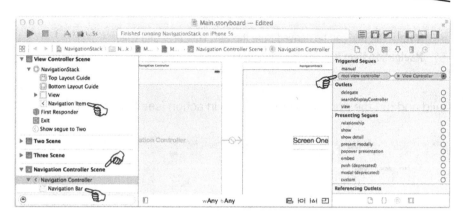

Figure 3-34. Navigation Controller scene and root view controller connection

4. Select the NavigationItem in Screen One to add title text (i.e., Navigation Stack), as shown in Figure 3-35.

   a. The title on the NavigationBar also affects the **Back** button title. iOS automatically updates the button title attribute to reflect where the **Back** button is going. The button text defaults to Back if the title is not assigned in the view.

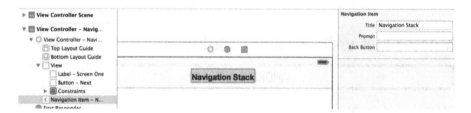

Figure 3-35. Title on the Navigation Item

Note The title on the Android Action bar is meant for the App identity. The iOS navigation bar title is more meant for the screen title.

5. Optional: The title and the rightBarButtonItem need to be installed on NavigationItem as you seen in previous step. If you want to set the title attribute or the rightBarButtonItem to Screen Two or Three, you need to add a NavigationItem to Screen Two or Three view controller first.

> **Note**   The title can be derived from the view controller title when
> **Navigation Item** is not being configured.

Build and run the app to see the live app in action (see Figure 3-36).

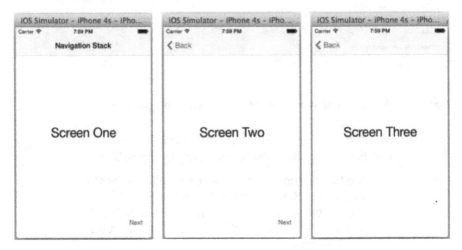

Figure 3-36. *The final NavigationStack app*

Master List with Details Drilldown

ANDROID ANALOGY

ListView and GridView.

Many apps need to display a list of items that users can tap to view more detailed information. They present a master list of items first, and the user selects one item to drill into.

This is probably one of the most common mobile navigation patterns. Both Android and iOS provide guidelines and offer system APIs to promote consistency by making the implementation easy for developers. In fact, both Xcode and ADT supply project templates for creating apps with this UX pattern.

In ADT, you can get the following master-detail app using the ADT **Master/Detail Flow** template. Initially, it presents the master list with three items. The app shows the detailed screen with the selected item content. You will port this app (see Figure 3-37) to the iOS platform.

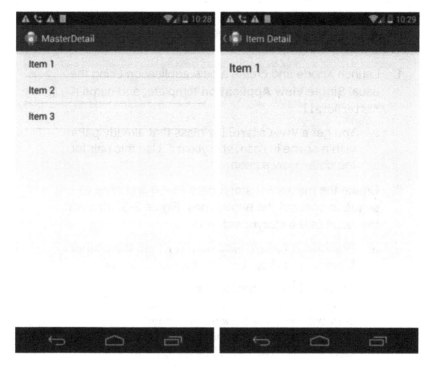

Figure 3-37. Android master list detailed drilldown

UITableViewController

ANDROID ANALOGY

The implementation concept appears very similar with different vocabularies:

- ListFragment = UITableViewController
- List View = Table View
- List View Item = Table View Cell
- List Adapter = Data Source

Even the adapter/data source implementations are sort of similar, too.

To port this Android app to iOS, you need two storyboard scenes: one for the master list and the other for the detailed content view. To have a fresh start, create a new iOS project:

1. Launch Xcode and create a new application using the usual **Single View Application** template, and name it MasterDetail.

    a. You get a ViewController class that already pairs with a scene in Main.storyboard. Use this pair for the detail view screen.

2. Create the master list storyboard scene and draw a segue to connect the two scenes. Figure 3-38 depicts the result of the storyboard work.

    a. Drag the UITableViewController from the **Object Library**, and drop it in the storyboard editor.

    b. Create a Manual Segue from the UITableViewController to the detailed view controller with the Show transition type (see Figure 3-25). Always give the segue an identifier, such as detail (see Figure 3-24).

3. Select the Table View Cell in the UITableViewController scene and open the **Attribute Inspector** to configure the Table View Cell (see pointers in Figure 3-38):

    a. Style: Select Basic (or others to see what they are in the editor).

    b. Identifier: Enter mycell. Always give it an identifier. You need it to create reusable cells, just as the Android recycled list item does.

    c. Accessory: Select Detail.

    d. Optionally, you may add an image that shows the icon on the left.

Figure 3-38. TableViewCell attributes

4. Embed the `UITableViewController` in a Navigation
    Controller (see Figure 3-33 in Navigation Stack). You
    normally use a Navigation Stack pattern for the screen
    transitions.

5. Check the **Is the Initial Scene** in the Navigation
    Controller **Attributes Inspector** (see Figure 3-39)
    to make the Navigation Controller the starting view
    controller of this app.

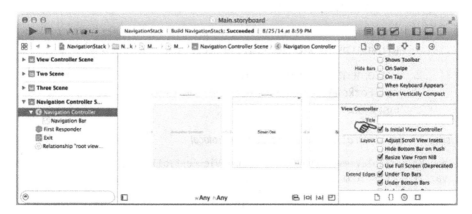

Figure 3-39. MasterDetail storyboard

6. Create a `MasterTableViewController` Swift class in the
    `ViewController.swift` file as shown in Listing 3-6.

    a. Subclass `MasterTableViewController` from
        `UITableViewController`.

    b. Pair this `MasterTableViewController` class with
        the Table View Controller scene in the **Identity
        Inspector** (see Figure 3-17).

Listing 3-6. MasterListTableViewController Class

```
class MasterTableViewController : UITableViewController {
  // TODO
}
```

> **Note**   In Swift, the class doesn't need to be in its own file. I choose to put
> in it the existing `ViewController.swift` file for no particular reason.
> If you are used to the Java way, you may create a new file to host this class.

UITableViewDataSource

ANDROID ANALOGY

android.widget.Adapter.

To populate the items in the Table View, you implement a Data Source: provide the TableViewCell with data by overriding the methods defined in the UITableViewDataSource protocol (see Listing 3-7). Do the following in the MasterDetail project:

1. Implement tableView(tableView,numberOfRowsInSection) to return number of items in the tableView.

2. Implement tableView(tableView, cellForRowAtIndexPath) to return the tableViewCell instance.

Listing 3-7. Implement UITableViewDataSource Protocol

```
class MasterTableViewController : UITableViewController {
  var items = ["item 1", "item 2", "item 3"]

  override func tableView(tableView: UITableView, numberOfRowsInSection
  section: Int) -> Int {
    return self.items.count
  }

  override func tableView(tableView: UITableView, cellForRowAtIndexPath
  indexPath: NSIndexPath) -> UITableViewCell {
    var cell = tableView.dequeueReusableCellWithIdentifier("mycell") as
    UITableViewCell
    cell.textLabel.text = self.items[indexPath.row]
    return cell
  }
}
```

> **Note** Use dequeueReusableCellWithIdentifier(...) to implement recycled views. This is a very common pattern for saving memory with a large amount of items, and iOS makes it easy by offering this method. Make sure you assign a cell identifier in storyboard.

UITableViewDelegate

```
ANDROID ANALOGY
```

ListFragment.onListItemClick(...).

To handle Table View item selected events, override the
UITableViewDelegate.tableView(tableView, didSelectRowAtIndexPath)
method (see Listing 3-8):

1. Implement UITableViewDelegate.
   didSelectRowAtIndexPath(...) to perform segues

2. Implement a prepareForSegue(...) callback to pass
   data to the detail view controller (see **Listing 3-5**
   for details).

Listing 3-8. Implementing UITableViewDelegate

```
class MasterTableViewController : UITableViewController {
  ...
  override func tableView(tableView: UITableView,
  didSelectRowAtIndexPath indexPath: NSIndexPath) {
    self.performSegueWithIdentifier("detail", sender: indexPath.row)
  }

  override func prepareForSegue(segue: UIStoryboardSegue,
  sender: AnyObject?) {
    var destVc = segue.destinationViewController as UIViewController
    destVc.navigationItem.title = self.items[sender as Int]
  }
}
```

3. To add or delete items, you need to explicitly refresh the
   table view:

   a. Drag and drop a **Bar Button Item** to the navigation
      bar and draw an IBAction to create the doAdd()
      method (Figure 3-40).

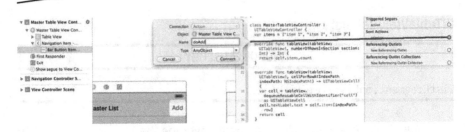

Figure 3-40. Navigation bar right button

b. To add an item when the Add button is selected, implement the doAdd() method as shown in Listing 3-9. Make sure you call TableView. reloadData() in the main thread to refresh the table view just like the notifyDataSetChanged() does in Android.

Listing 3-9. Refresh Table View

```
class MasterTableViewController : UITableViewController {
  var items = ["item 1", "item 2", "item 3"]

  @IBAction func doAdd(sender: AnyObject) {
    self.items.append("item \(self.items.count + 1)")
    self.tableView.reloadData()
  }
  ...
```

Build and run (⌘+R) the app to see the MasterDetail iOS app live in action (see Figure 3-41).

Figure 3-41. MasterDetail app screens in iOS

UITableView

ANDROID ANALOGY

android.widget.ListView.

Just like the Android ListFragment class, which is a Fragment containing a ListView, UITableViewController is a regular UIViewController with a pre-wired tableView in it. You will have the same choice to make: whether or not to use UITableViewController, which simplifies some coding for you (actually not that much, IMO). More often, I choose to do the following instead of using UITableViewController:

1. In storyboard, create a regular View Controller with TableView:

   a. Add a regular ViewController scene.

   b. Add a TableView to the scene. This gives you more flexibility (i.e., to draw the table view at any location).

   c. Connect the table view to an IBOutlet (see Figure 3-20 for details).

   d. Select the TableView and connect delegate and dataSource outlets to the ViewController in **Connection Inspector**.

2. Create a Swift class to pair with the content view:

   a. Subclass from the regular UIViewController class.

   b. Implement UITableViewDataSource and UITableViewDelegate protocols.

The previous MasterTableViewController is essentially equivalent to the code in Listing 3-10, and you still implement the same methods declared in UITableViewDataSource and UITableViewDelegate.

Listing 3-10. Explicitly Implement Table View Protocols

```
class MasterTableViewController : UIViewController, UITableViewDataSource,
UITableViewDelegate {
  @IBOutlet weak var tableView: UITableView!
  ...
```

UITableViewCell

```
ANDROID ANALOGY
```

`R.id.simple_list_item_1` from Android SDK, or create custom list item layout.

Similar to Android list-view item usages, you get some free types of `UITableViewCell` that you can select from iOS SDK. Previously in the `MasterDetail` project, we selected the **Basic** style, which gives you one `textLabel` in the Table View cell (see Figure 3-38). **Right Details**, **Left Details**, or **Subtitle** styles all give you a second label called `detailedTextLabel`. You can also set a left image icon and other `TableViewCell` attributes as shown in Figure 3-38.

You may programmatically configure `TableViewCell` using the `tableView` (`cellForRowAtIndexPath`) method. Listing 3-11 shows a typical example:

Listing 3-11. TableViewCell Properties

```
override func tableView(tableView: UITableView, cellForRowAtIndexPath
indexPath: NSIndexPath) -> UITableViewCell {
    var cell = ...
    cell.textLabel.text = self.items[indexPath.row]
    cell.detailTextLabel.text = "some detail label"
    cell.imageView.image = UIImage(named: "pointer.png")
    cell.accessoryType = UITableViewCellAccessoryType.DetailButton
    return cell
}
```

You can also choose "**Custom**" style, and draw the cell freely using storyboard; you will do so in the next section.

UICollectionView

```
ANDROID ANALOGY
```

`GridView.`

In Android, `GridView` is just a variant of the master-detail drilldown pattern using a different UI widget to show the master list. However, on tablets or large-screen devices, `GridView` is widely used due to greater space efficiencies that use multiple columns to organize the master list items, rather than a simple one-dimensional list. On iOS platforms, `UICollectionView` comes to the rescue.

It would be a shame if you didn't try this variant right now, because it is a really useful widget that takes very little extra effort. The key is the UICollectionView class.

> **Note** You can also use UICollectionViewController, which contains a UICollectionView that occupies the whole scene by default. Same choice: UITableViewController versus UITableView, which we discussed earlier (see "UITableView" section).

The MasterDetail project you created fits comfortably on an iPhone, but when it is running in iPad, it feels like the space is not being utilized efficiently. Create a new Xcode project using UICollectionView to demonstrate the usage:

1. Launch Xcode and create a new application using the usual **Single View Application** template. Name it MasterGridDetail.

    a. You get a scene in the Main.storyboard and a ViewController class pair.

    b. Rename the class to MasterViewController in both the ViewController.swift file and as the custom class name of the view controller scene (see Figure 3-17).

    c. Drag a Collection View from the **Object Library** and drop it onto the MasterViewController scene. Let it take up the whole space and pin **zero** spacing to Superview in all four directions from the Xcode menu bar at **Editor ➤ Pin ➤ ...** .

    d. Embed the MasterViewController controller in the Navigation Controller (see Figure 3-33)

2. Select the Collection View in storyboard to create connections in **Connections Inspector** as shown in Figure 3-42:

    a. Connect dataSource and delegate outlets to the MasterViewController.

    b. Open **Assistant Editor** and connect **New Referencing Outlet** to MasterViewController property. Name it mCollectionView.

Figure 3-42. *Collection View dataSource, delegate, and IBOutlet connections*

3. Draw your own custom collection view cell in storyboard:

    a. In **Attributes Inspector**, assign **Collection Reusable View Cell Identifier** a value (i.e., mycell). There are some attributes you can change safely in the **Attributes Inspector**, such as the **white** background color.

    b. To change the size of the cell, select the parent collection view and change the cell size to **150 × 150** in **Size Inspector**. Figure 3-43 shows other measurements that you can set.

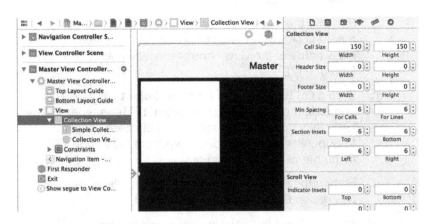

Figure 3-43. *Size Inspector*

    c. Add a Label to the cell, make the font size bigger (i.e., **30**), center alignment, and add Auto Layout constraints as shown in Figure 3-44.

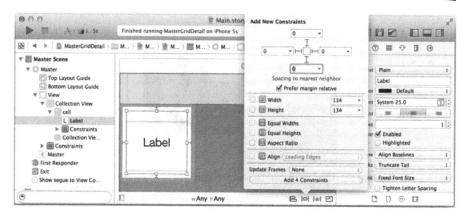

Figure 3-44. Drawing the collection view cell

4. Create a custom Swift class for the collection view cell. Listing 3-12 shows the `SimpleCollectionViewCell` class:

    a. Create a swift class, `SimpleCollectionViewCell`, subclassed from `UICollectionViewCell`.

    b. Select the collection view cell in storyboard and assign the `SimpleCollectionViewCell` class in **Identity Inspector**.

    c. Open the **Assistant Editor** with the `SimpleCollectionViewCell` class. In the **Connections Inspector**, connect the **Referencing Outlet** to create an IBOutlet, and name it `textLabel`.

Listing 3-12. SimpleCollectionViewCell class

```
class SimpleCollectionViewCell : UICollectionViewCell {
  @IBOutlet weak var textLabel: UILabel!
}
```

5. Create the detail view controller scene in storyboard as shown Figure 3-45:

    a. Add a regular view controller from the **Object Library**.

    b. Create a manual segue from the Master View Controller scene to the detailed view controller with a Show transition type (see Figure 3-25). Always enter a storyboard segue **Identifier** (i.e., detail).

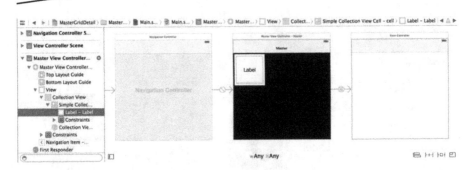

Figure 3-45. Creating the detail view controller in MasterDetail storyboard

6. MasterViewController must implement
    UICollectionViewDataSource and
    UICollectionViewDelegate protocols (see Listing 3-13):

    a. Implement numberOfSectionsInCollectionView
        (collectionView) to return the section number; it
        defaults to 1 if not implemented.

    b. Implement collectionView(collectionView,
        numberOfItemsInSection) to return number of items
        in each section.

    c. Implement collectionView(collectionView,
        cellForItemAtIndexPath) to return the collection
        view cell instance.

    d. Implement collectionView(collectionView,
        didSelectItemAtIndexPath) to respond to cell
        selection.

Listing 3-13. UICollectionViewDataSource and UICollectionViewDelegate Protocols

```
class MasterViewController : UIViewController, UICollectionViewDataSource,
UICollectionViewDelegate {
  ...
  // implement UICollectionViewDataSource
  var items = ["item 1", "item 2", "item 3", "item 4", "item 5", "item 6",
  "item 7"]
  func collectionView(collectionView: UICollectionView,
  numberOfItemsInSection section: Int) -> Int {
    return self.items.count
  }
```

```
// The cell that is returned must be retrieved from a call to -dequeueReus
   ableCellWithReuseIdentifier:forIndexPath:
func collectionView(collectionView: UICollectionView,
cellForItemAtIndexPath indexPath: NSIndexPath) -> UICollectionViewCell {
  var cell = collectionView.dequeueReusableCellWithReuseIdentifier("cell",
  forIndexPath: indexPath) as SimpleCollectionViewCell
  cell.textLabel.text = self.items[indexPath.row]
  cell.backgroundColor = (indexPath.row % 2 == 0) ? UIColor.whiteColor() :
  UIColor.lightGrayColor()
  return cell
}

func numberOfSectionsInCollectionView(collectionView: UICollectionView)
-> Int {
  return 1
}

// implement UICollectionViewDelegate
func collectionView(collectionView: UICollectionView,
didSelectItemAtIndexPath indexPath: NSIndexPath) {
  self.performSegueWithIdentifier("detail", sender: self)
}
}
```

Both TableView and CollectionView are very versatile. You should look into the data source and delegate protocols to see the rich options offered to developers. Build and run the MasterGridDetail iOS app to see your code live in action as shown in Figure 3-46.

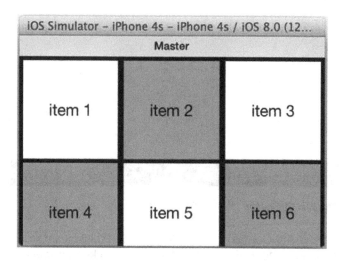

Figure 3-46. Collection view

Navigation Tabs

Navigation tabs are another popular UX design pattern. Apple's iOS Human Interface Guidelines suggest using a tab bar to give users access to different perspectives on the same set of data or on different subtasks related to the overall function of your app. Each navigation tab is associated with a view controller. When the user selects a specific tab, the associated view controller presents its own content view.

In Android, you normally use **Actionbar**. Figure 3-47 shows an example; let's translate it to iOS.

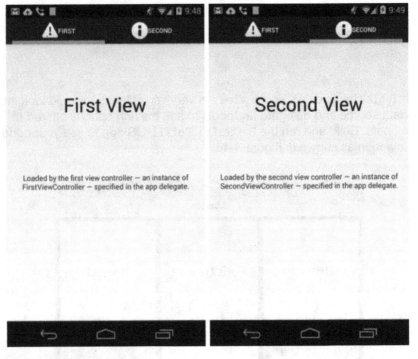

Figure 3-47. Android TabbedApp

The key in iOS is the Container View Controller, `UITabBarController` class. You can use it as is most of the time. If you want to keep some application states in the Container View Controller, simply subclass from it.

Implementing Navigation Tabs

The following instructions walk you through the steps you normally take to implement navigation tabs:

1. Launch Xcode to create a new app using **Single View Application** template, and name it TabbedApp.

   a. You get an empty scene in the Main.storyboard and a ViewController class.

   b. Rename the class to FirstViewController in both the ViewController.swift file and the class name in **Identity Inspector** for the storyboard scene.

   c. Draw the content view in the storyboard scene using the Android app as your wireframe.

2. You need the second content view and view controller pair.

   a. You can copy, paste, and modify from the FirstViewController class. Listing 3-14 shows the SecondViewController class.

Listing 3-14. SecondViewController Class

```
class SecondViewController: UIViewController {
  ...
}
```

   b. You can copy, paste, and modify the storyboard scene in the storyboard editor, too. Don't forget to update the class name in **Identify Inspector**. Figure 3-48 shows that the storyboard has the Screen One and Screen Two scenes.

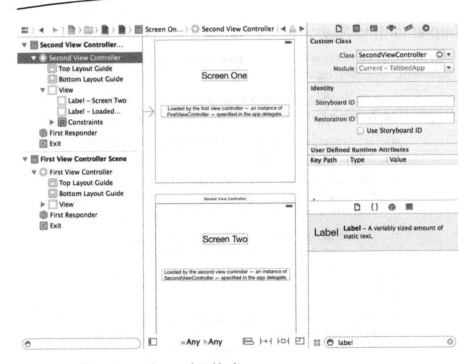

Figure 3-48. First and second scenes in TabbedApp

3.   Add a Container View Controller, `UITabBarController`, which will be responsible for managing the two content view controllers.

   a.   Embed both storyboard scenes in a `TabBarController`: multiselect both storyboard scenes (press and hold the ⌘ key for multiselect) and select the command from **Editor ➤ Embed In ➤ Tab Bar Controller** in the Xcode menu bar (see Figure 3-49).

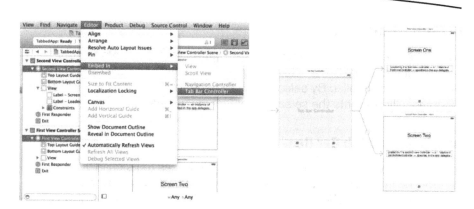

Figure 3-49. Embed content views in Tab Bar Controller (the result on the right)

The app is not complete yet, but you actually can run it now to see the app live (see Figure 3-50).

Figure 3-50. TabbedApp draft

UITabBarController

As you can see from previous work (see Figure 3-49), a bottom tab bar comes with UITabBarController. Each tab bar item is associated with a content view controller. By selecting a tab bar item, the UITabBarController automatically presents the selected content view controller.

Add/Remove a Tab Bar Item

UITabBarController maintains an array of references to its child view controllers. In its **Connections Inspector**, you can draw a view controller's outlet in the Triggered Segues section to add the child view controllers to the UITabBarController.viewControllers array property. You can write code to add or remove the child view controller in the runtime, too.

Update the Look and Feel of the Tab Bar Items

You should assign a title and an image to the tab bar items. When a UIViewController is added to a tab bar controller, the UIViewController. tabBarItem property represents the tab bar item in the tab bar. You assign appropriate values in the tab bar item's **Attributes Inspector**. In the runtime, you use code to update the text and image by setting appropriate tabBarItem properties. Previously, Figure 3-50 shows two tab bar items with the same label and without an icon image. Do the following to give our TabbedApp a better look:

1. System provides a set of common tab bar items
    (**System Item** in **Attributes Inspector**). Use them when possible for consistent platform convention. Select the **Featured** system item for Screen One (see Figure 3-51).

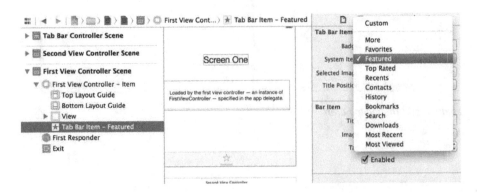

Figure 3-51. Adding the Featured System Item to Screen One

2. For Screen Two, select **Custom** to supply your own tab bar item **Title** and **Image icon** (see Figure 3-52).

    a. Enter the Title (e.g., **Two**).

    b. Create an image icon in images.xcassets (i.e., tab1), and drop a transparent PNG with size about **25 × 25** (max **48 × 32**). The icon color is not required, as only the alpha channel is to be rendered.

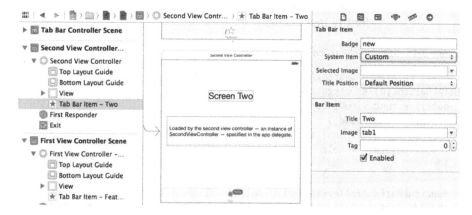

Figure 3-52. Custom tab item with badgeValue

Note   iOS is very picky about the right image specs. See the online reference for image specs: https://developer.apple.com/ library/ios/documentation/UserExperience/Conceptual/ MobileHIG/IconMatrix.html.

---

c. Enter the Image name (e.g., tab1).

d. You may enter a **badge** (e.g., **New**), which will appear on the upper right corner of the icon. Frequently, it is set programmatically in the runtime using the UITabbatItem.badgeValue property.

Handle Runtime Behavior

To respond to the runtime behavior programatically, just like most of the UIKit widgets, you implement a delegate protocol: UITabBarDelegate. Continue with the TabbedApp to learn the common tasks for handling UITabBarDelegate runtime events.

1. Create a custom tab bar controller to handle runtime behaviors as shown in Listing 3-15:

    a. Create a `SimpleTabBarController` class subclassing from `UITabBarController`.

    b. Declare `SimpleTabBarController` to implement `UITabBarControllerDelegate` protocol.

    c. In storyboard, select the tab bar controller and assign the `SimpleTabBarController` class in the **Identity Inspector**.

Listing 3-15. `SimpleTabBarController` Class

```
class SimpleTabBarController : UITabBarController,
UITabBarControllerDelegate {
  override func viewDidLoad() {
    super.viewDidLoad()
    // Do any additional setup after loading the view ...
    self.delegate = self
  }

  func tabBarController(tabBarController: UITabBarController,
  shouldSelectViewController viewController: UIViewController) -> Bool {
    // you may do something and return true
    // Or, return false to not to select viewController
    return true
  }

  func tabBarController(tabBarController: UITabBarController,
  didSelectViewController viewController: UIViewController) {
    // you may do something
  }
}
```

2. Each child content view controller can access `UIViewController.tabBarController` and `UIViewController.tabBarItem` properties. Listing 3-16 shows how to change the second tab's `badgeValue` from the `FirstViewController`.

Listing 3-16. Change badgeValue of Other tabBarItem

```
(self.tabBarController!.viewControllers![1] as
  UIViewController).tabBarItem.badgeValue = "Zzz"
```

By the way, the tab bar is located on the bottom screen in iOS instead of at the top in Android. In general, platform-specific UX guidelines should never be overlooked. Keep the navigation bar on the bottom in iOS, which is where most iOS users expect it.

Swipe Views

The Carousel is a popular UX pattern commonly used in many platforms, including desktop and web apps. On mobile platforms, you use this pattern with swipe gestures to display content, page by page. It allows the user to move from item to item efficiently. With animated transitions, it offers a more enjoyable viewing experience. Both iOS and Android provide framework classes, as well as a project creation template to promote this navigation UX pattern.

In Android, you normally use the ViewPager widget. Figure 3-53 shows the Android SwipeViews app that was created using the ADT Swipe View template:

- The container Activity has a ViewPager to show the swipeable views from a fragment layout.

- It has one fragment that contains a label that represents the page content.

- The pager adapter creates the fragment with content for each page.

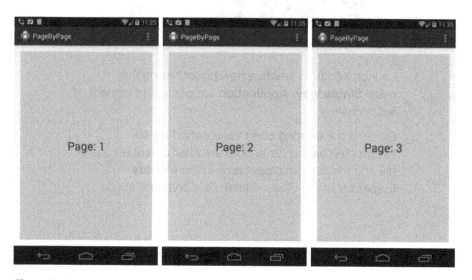

Figure 3-53. Android SwipeViews app

You will port this to iOS. Use the Android app or layout file (see Figure 3-54) as the wireframe to construct the storyboard scenes to start with.

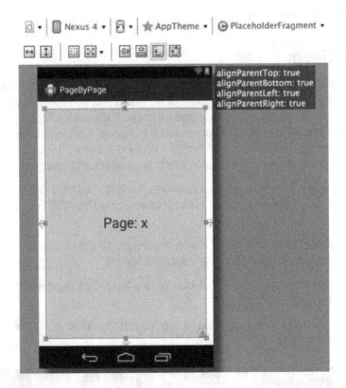

Figure 3-54. Android `layout.xml` file

1. Launch Xcode to create a new project using the usual **Single View Application** template, and name it SwipeViews.

2. Rename the existing class ViewController to ParentViewController in both the ViewController.swift file and the custom class name in the **Identity Inspector** of the view controller's storyboard scene.

3. Drag and drop a UIView onto the storyboard scene from **Object Library**:

    a. Open the storyboard **Assistant Editor** and create an IBOutlet in **Connections Inspector** by connecting the referencing outlet to the paired view controller, and name it mPageView.

    b. Add Auto Layout constraints to **pin** the edges to nearest neighbors and set the background to be light gray, as shown in the final storyboard (see Figure 3-55).

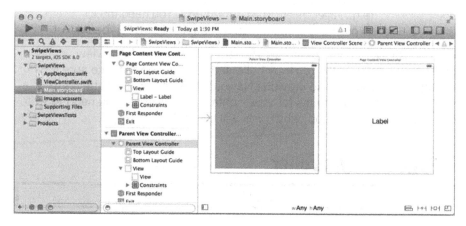

Figure 3-55. Main.storyboard in SwipeViews project

4. You need another content view–view controller pair for the page content.

    a. Create a new PageContentViewController class (see Listing 3-17).

Listing 3-17. Two Classes in ViewController.swift File

```swift
import UIKit
class ParentViewController : UIViewController {
  @IBOutlet weak var mPageView: UIView!

  override func viewDidLoad() {
    super.viewDidLoad()
  }
```

```
  override func didReceiveMemoryWarning() {
    super.didReceiveMemoryWarning()
    // Dispose of any resources that can be recreated.
  }
}

class PageContentViewController: UIViewController {
  @IBOutlet weak var textLabel : UILabel
}
```

      b.   Draw the second storyboard scene (see the screen on
          the right in Figure 3-55). Make sure you give the
          Page Content View controller a **storyboard ID**
          (e.g., PageContentViewController). You need the ID
          to programmatically load a controller from storyboard.

Nothing is new yet; just draw two storyboard scenes with the view
controllers to start with. You may build and run the app to make sure it
contains no errors. Unlike previous Navigation Stack or Tab patterns to
which you can draw segues for view controller transitions, you need to write
code to complete the app, which you will do next.

UIPageViewController

ANDROID ANALOGY

ViewPager.

The key to implementing the swipe view pattern in iOS is the
UIPageViewController class, which uses the same data source pattern:
implement a data source that is responsible for providing content views
populated with data. Continue with the folowing steps in the SwipeViews
Xcode project:

    1.   Modify the PageContentViewController class so it can
        receive data and present the three simple screens (see
        Listing 3-18).

Listing 3-18. Add data and pageNo Properties

```
class PageContentViewController: UIViewController {

  @IBOutlet weak var textLabel : UILabel
```

```
var data = ""
var pageNo = 0

override func viewDidLoad() {
  self.textLabel.text = data
}
}
```

2. UIPageViewController works with dataSource
   and delegate protocol. The parent view controller,
   ParentViewController, is a legitimate candidate for
   implementing them (see Listing 3-19).

   a. UIPageViewControllerDataSource is responsible for
      supplying the content view controller before and
      after the current content one.

   b. UIPageViewControllerDataSource also defines the
      optional page count and page selection indicator.

   c. UIPageViewControllerDelegate defines the optional
      page controller events callbacks.

Listing 3-19. ParentViewController Implements dataSource and delegate Protocol

```
class ParentViewController : UIViewController,
UIPageViewControllerDataSource, UIPageViewControllerDelegate {

  ...
  // implement data source
  let items = ["Page: 1", "Page: 2", "Page: 3"]
  func pageViewController(pageViewController: UIPageViewController,
  viewControllerBeforeViewController viewController: UIViewController) ->
  UIViewController? {

    var pageNo = (viewController as PageContentViewController).pageNo
    if pageNo > 0 {
      var vc = self.storyboard.
      instantiateViewControllerWithIdentifier("PageContentViewController")
      as PageContentViewController
      vc.data = self.items[pageNo-1]
      vc.pageNo = pageNo - 1
      return vc
    }

    return nil
  }
```

```
func pageViewController(pageViewController: UIPageViewController,
viewControllerAfterViewController viewController: UIViewController) ->
UIViewController? {

  var pageNo = (viewController as PageContentViewController).pageNo
  if pageNo < self.items.count - 1 {
    var vc = self.storyboard.
    instantiateViewControllerWithIdentifier("PageContentViewController")
    as PageContentViewController
    vc.data = self.items[pageNo+1]
    vc.pageNo = pageNo + 1
    return vc
  }

  return nil
}

func presentationCountForPageViewController(pageViewController:
UIPageViewController) -> Int {
  return self.items.count
}
func presentationIndexForPageViewController(pageViewController:
UIPageViewController) -> Int {
  return (pageViewController.viewControllers[0] as
  PageContentViewController).pageNo
}

}
```

3. In the ParentViewController viewDidLoad() method,
    the following conventional code (see Listing 3-20) sets
    up the UIPageViewController:

    a. Initialize page view controller.

    b. Set up the dataSource and delegate.

    c. Set the first page view controller.

    d. Establish the parent-child view controller hierarchy.

Listing 3-20. Setting Up UIPageViewController in viewDidLoad

```
class ParentViewController : UIViewController,
UIPageViewControllerDataSource, UIPageViewControllerDelegate {

  @IBOutlet weak var mPageView: UIView
  var mPageViewController: UIPageViewController
```

```
override func viewDidLoad() {
  super.viewDidLoad()
  // Do any additional setup after loading the view, typically from a nib.

  // a. initialize page view controller, view and gestures
  self.mPageViewController = UIPageViewController(transitionStyle:
  UIPageViewControllerTransitionStyle.Scroll, navigationOrientation:
  UIPageViewControllerNavigationOrientation.Horizontal, options: nil)
  self.mPageViewController.view.frame = self.mPageView.bounds
  self.mPageView.gestureRecognizers = self.mPageViewController.
  gestureRecognizers

  // b. set data source and delegate
  self.mPageViewController.delegate = self
  self.mPageViewController.dataSource = self

  // c. set the first page
  var vc = self.storyboard.
  instantiateViewControllerWithIdentifier("PageContentViewController") as
  PageContentViewController
  vc.data = self.items[0]
  vc.pageNo = 0
  self.mPageViewController.setViewControllers([vc], direction: .Forward,
  animated: false, completion: nil)

  // d. establish parent-child view and view controller hierachy
  self.mPageView.addSubview(self.mPageViewController.view)
  self.addChildViewController(self.mPageViewController)
  self.mPageViewController.didMoveToParentViewController(self)
}
```

This is all about the UIPageViewController class and the Swipe View navigation pattern in iOS. Build and run the iOS SwipeViews app to see your code in action (see Figure 3-56).

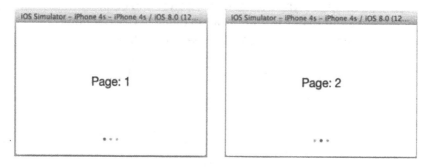

Figure 3-56. iOS SwipeViews app

Dialogs

Generally, you use the Dialogs UX pattern to give mobile users quick feedback or to request simple confirmation of choices. Dialogs normally sit on top of the current screen while that screen remains partially visible or dimmed. This creates a visual effect that is meant to get more user attention without losing the current context.

Create an Xcode project to demonstrate the uses of Dialogs and common programming tasks:

1. Launch Xcode to create a new project using the **Single View Application** template, and name it `Dialogs`.

2. Draw two `Button` widgets with titles set to `Alert` and `Popup` in the storyboard scene as shown in Figure 3-57.

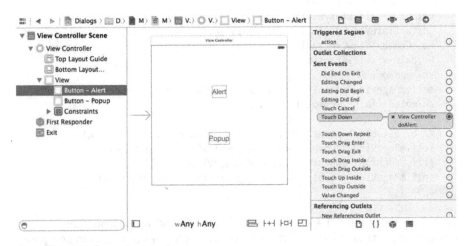

Figure 3-57. Dialogs storyboard

3. Open the storyboard **Assistant Editor** and connect the **Send Event ➤ Touch Down** outlet in **Connections Inspector** to create `IBAction` methods in the paired `ViewController` class for both buttons (see `doAlert(...)` and `doPopup(...)` in Listing 3-21).

Listing 3-21. Create IBAction methods for the Alert and Popup buttons

```
import UIKit
class ViewController: UIViewController, UIAlertViewDelegate {
  ...
  @IBAction func doAlert(sender: AnyObject) {
    // TODO
  }
  @IBAction func doPopup(sender: AnyObject) {
    // TODO
  }
}
```

Nothing should be new to you here, but this `Dialogs` Xcode project should give you a refresher on dialog topics.

UIAlertController

```
ANDROID ANALOGY
```

`AlertDialog.`

Figure 3-58 shows the standard Android and iOS alert dialogs side by side. On iOS, you use `UIAlertController`. The basic usages are almost identical except the extra title icon on the Android `AlertDialog`.

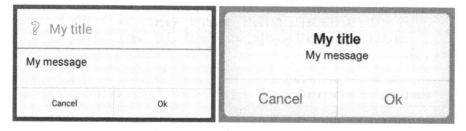

Figure 3-58. Android (left) vs. iOS (right) alert dialogs

Contiune with the Xcode Dialogs project and add the following code to learn the UIAlertController code:

1. To show the iOS dialog as depicted in Figure 3-58, add the following code in the ViewController.doAlert(...) method (see Listing 3-22):

    a. Create a UIAlertController instance.

    b. Add UIAlertAction for dialog buttons.

    c. To prompt user input, add TextField to UIAlertController.

    d. Use the regular UIViewController API to present it as a view controller.

Listing 3-22. Present UIAlertController

```
@IBAction func doAlert(sender: AnyObject) {

  var alert = UIAlertController(title: "My title", message: "My message",
  preferredStyle: UIAlertControllerStyle.Alert)

  // add action buttons
  var actionCancel = UIAlertAction(title: "Cancel", style:
  UIAlertActionStyle.Cancel,
    handler: {action in
      // do nothing
    })

  var actionOk = UIAlertAction(title: "Ok",
  style: UIAlertActionStyle.Default, handler: {action in
      println((alert.textFields[0] as UITextField).text)
    })

  alert.addAction(actionCancel)
  alert.addAction(actionOk)

  // add text fields
  alert.addTextFieldWithConfigurationHandler({textField in
    // config the UITextField
    textField.backgroundColor = UIColor.yellowColor()
    textField.placeholder = "enter text, i.e., Do Ra Me"
    })

  // UIViewController API to presend viewController
  self.presentViewController(alert, animated: true, completion: nil)
}
```

Everything inside the UIAlertController is created programatically. Figure 3-59 shows the UIAlertController code live in action.

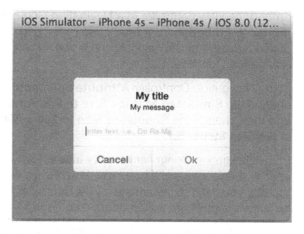

Figure 3-59. iOS UIAlertController

UIPopoverController

```
                    ANDROID ANALOGY
```

DialogFragment.

On iOS devices with large screens such as the iPad, you can use PopoverController to present a regular viewController as a popover. The popover can be anchored at a given position to associate the presented dialog with the presenting context. On devices with compact size classes such as the iPhone, the popover controller automatically falls back to the regular full-screen view controller. You can also take advantage of the storyboard editor to draw the content views and segue instead of writing code.

The following steps demonstrate the PopoverController in the Dialogs project:

1. Add a new storyboard scene for the popover.

    a. Create a GreenViewController class as shown in Listing 3-23 and draw a view controller scene in storyboard to pair with it by specifying the class name in **Identity Inspector**.

Listing 3-23. GreenViewController Class

```
class GreenViewController : UIViewController {
  @IBAction func doDone(sender: AnyObject) {
    // do something and dismiss
    self.dismissViewControllerAnimated(true, completion:nil)
  }
}
```

b. Embed the view controller in a Navigation Controller
    (**Editor ➤ Embed in** from the Xcode menu bar) to
    take advantage of the navigation bar title, or any
    Navigation Controller features.

c. In the Navigation Controller **Attributes Inspector**,
    change the **Simulated Metrics Size** to **Freeform**,
    and then change the **Simulated Size** to **250 × 300**
    in the **Size Inspector**.

d. In the Navigation Controller **Identity Inspector**,
    specify the Storyboard ID, i.e., nav. You always need
    the ID if you want to instantiate a view controller
    instance directly from a storyboard (see Listing 3-24).

e. You normally draw meaningful contents in content
    view. For simplicity, use the **Attributes Inspector**
    to change the GreenViewController view's
    Background attribute to be **Green**.

f. Draw a BarButtonItem on the right side of navigation
    bar in the GreenViewController, and connect the
    Send Actions outlet to the IBAction method in
    GreenViewController as shown in Listing 3-23.
    Figure 3-60 depicts the completed storyboard.

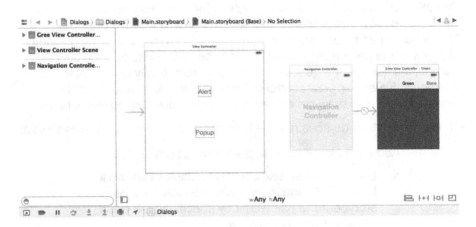

Figure 3-60. Dialogs storyboard completion

2. To present the GreenViewController, draw a Manual Segue from the presenting ViewController to the parent Navigation Controller of GreenViewController. Specify the segue attributes value as shown in **Attributes Inspector** in Figure 3-61.

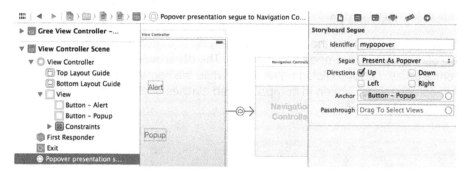

Figure 3-61. Storyboard segue attributes in the Attributes Inspector

 a. Identifier: mypopover.

 b. Segue type: Present As Popover.

 c. Direction: Up (you may play with other values).

 d. Anchor outlet: Drag the outlet to the Popup button in the presenting view controller.

3. To perform the mypopover Manual Segue, update the ViewController.doPopup(...) IBAction method as shown in Listing 3-24. Note that the commented code programmatically presents a UIPopoverController without using the storyboard segue.

Listing 3-24. Perform the mypopover Manual Segue

```
// In ViewController class
@IBAction func doPopup(sender: AnyObject) {
  self.performSegueWithIdentifier("mypopover", sender: nil)

// var nav = self.storyboard.instantiateViewControllerWithIdentifier("nav")
    as UIViewController
// var popover = UIPopoverController(contentViewController: nav)
// popover.delegate = self;
// popover.popoverContentSize = nav.view.bounds.size
// popover.presentPopoverFromRect(self.mPopupButton.frame, inView: self.view,
    permittedArrowDirections: UIPopoverArrowDirection.Up, animated: true)
}
```

4. You may dismiss the popover by tapping anywhere inside the presenting view controller but outside the GreenViewController content view. To dismiss the popover programmatically, implement GreenViewController.doDone(...) to call the dismissViewControllerAnimated(...) as shown in Listing 3-23.

You can build and run the Xcode Dialogs project to see the UIPopoverController code live in action. The UIPopoverController is rendered as a popup dialog on an iPad, while the same code renders a full-screen modal screen in compact-sized classes such as the iPhone, as shown in Figure 3-62.

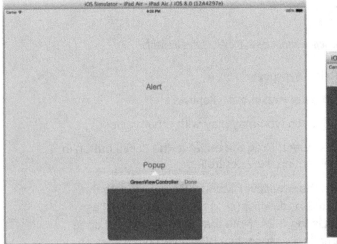

Figure 3-62. The results of the UIPopoverController code on the iPad vs. the iPhone

Toasts

For giving users quick feedback, which dismisses automatically, you normally use Toast in Android apps. There is no Android-like Toast widget in iOS. I really like it, but it probably would look Android-ish on iOS. You can always create a small view area with fade-in and fade-out effects programmatically with a timer.

Summary

To port Android to an iOS app, first create storyboard scenes using the counterpart Android app as the wireframe to break your app naturally into a structured MVC project in a top-down fashion. The result is a set of content view–view controller pairs that map to the Android counterpart layout-fragment pairs.

Next, to implement the screen navigation patterns, you draw storyboard segues to connect storyboard scenes. You also choose the appropriate container view controller (i.e., UINavigationController) from SDK to facilitate the screen transitions. The remaining content view and view controller mappings between iOS and Android are trivial. You will dive into the details of each screen in Chapter 4.

Chapter **4**

Implement Piece by Piece

In the previous chapter, you started with iOS storyboard to lay down the groundwork using navigation patterns. It resulted in a set of connected `UIViewController` classes set in an MVC framework that mapped to Android counterpart fragments.

In this chapter, you are going to implement each view-controller pair, one piece at a time, with a detailed user interface and business logic that should already be present in the counterpart Android `Fragment` and the layout file. You will also focus on the following common programming-task mappings from iOS to Android:

- User interface and common UI widgets
- Persistent storage options
- Network and remote services with JSON

User Interface

All those storyboard scenes that you implemented using the screen navigation patterns in Chapter 3 were intentionally very simple. Obviously, a useful mobile app provides rich content and offers better functionality to gracefully interact with users. The user interface will certainly play an important role in the overall user experience.

The techniques and vocabularies for creating meaningful user interfaces for iOS are definitely different from those for Android. UI components are normally platform dependent. You just need to know the usages of the UI widgets and where to look up the platform-specific widget specifications.

On the other hand, there are similarities among many UI frameworks. Both iOS and Android view blocks are structured as a view container (view/parent) model, which has been in the industry for a long time. In iOS, UIView is an object that draws something on the screen with which the user can interact. A UIView is also a container that holds other UIView objects to define the hierarchical layout of the UI.

The view container model appears similar to Android but with differences in how to position a UI widget within its parent view or relative to siblings. Android uses **layout managers**, whereas iOS uses **auto layout**.

UIView

The UIView object is the basic building block for UI components. It is the base class for all widgets, such as common widgets like UIButton and UILabel. It is also used as the parent container view.

ANDROID ANALOGY

android.view.View or android.view.ViewGroup.

A visible UIView occupies a rectangular area on the screen and is responsible for drawing and event handling. The UIViewController class has a root view defined in the UIViewController.view property that is inherited by all the view controllers. All UI widgets are special types of UIView that have attributes for the intended look, feel, and behaviors. When drawing the view elements in storyboard, they are added to the parent view, and you use the storyboard view **Inspectors** to visually edit the view properties.

All the iOS UI widgets inherit from UIView. You can set the inherited UIView attributes in the storyboard view **Attributes Inspector**. For example, Figure 4-1 depicts the View section in the **Attributes Inspector** for any UI widgets.

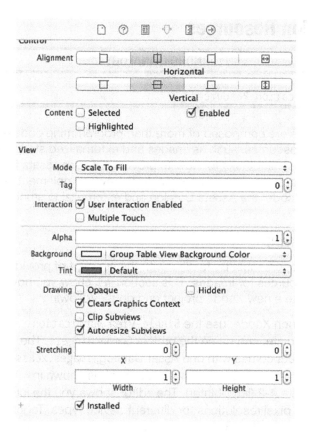

Figure 4-1. *View section of Attributes Inspector*

At runtime, you can programmatically update these properties of the UIView object. UIView is the ultimate super class of all the widgets. It offers a fairly rich API for developers to implement a number of UI related responsibilities:

- rendering content

- layout and manage subviews

- event handling

- animations

The rest of the chapter demonstrates the common attributes or APIs that you most likely will encounter or that are just good to know beforehand. Before diving into common iOS UI widgets from the iOS SDK, I want to talk about an important related topic, **Application Resources**, which will be used by UI widgets as well as many other common programming tasks.

Application Resources

ANDROID ANALOGY

Android Application Resources

Most GUI apps are composed of more than programming code—they require other resources, such as images and externalized strings. In iOS, you will encounter similar tasks for how to provide different assets for different device configurations. This will demonstrate how to implement two common use cases in Xcode: the Assets Catalog and externalizing strings.

Assets Catalog

Android developers must be familiar with the concept of providing alternative resources for images. This section will show you how in iOS. As usual, create a new Xcode project and do the following:

1. Launch Xcode, use the Single View Application template, and name the project CommonWidgets. The project comes with one Asset Catalog, Images.xcassets, that already contains the AppIcon set as shown in Figure 4-2 (left pointer). The editor shows you the icons and pixel resolutions for different device types. Toggle the **iOS 6.1 and Prior Sizes** check box (right pointer in Figure 4-2) to see the differences in the editor.

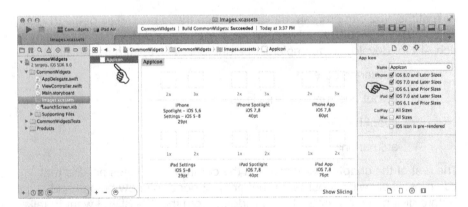

Figure 4-2. AppIcon set in Images.xcassets

2. You can recreate the icons from the Android counterpart, `res/drawable-xxhdpi/ic_launcher.png`, with the different image resolutions specified in the editor. Drag and drop the appropriate image files on the guided squares. Figure 4-3 depicts the result.

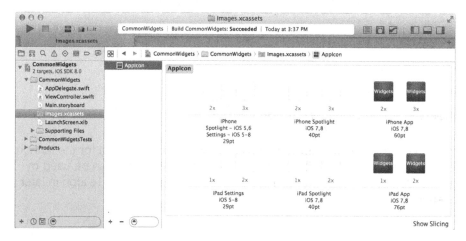

Figure 4-3. *Recreating Android icons in iOS with* `Images.xcassets`

3. To add an image asset, click the **Add** (+) button and select **New Image Set** as shown in Figure 4-4:

   a. Use the **Attributes Inspector** to select the type of devices you want to provide.

   b. You may choose to supply the image set by selecting the **Universal** size class or device-specific types. Either way, 1x, 2x, and 3x should cover all the iOS devices now.

   c. Select the image with 1x resolution and drop it on the right spot (as shown by the pointer under **sample** in Figure 4-4). Repeat the step for 2x and 3x images.

   d. Give the Image Set a name (e.g., `sample`). The name is the identifier to access the image from your code or from storyboard.

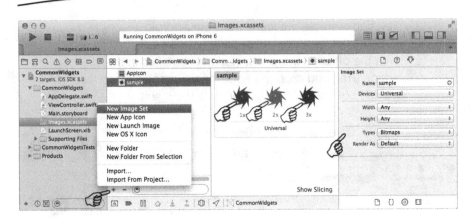

Figure 4-4. *Adding an image set in* `Images.xcassets`

You have created two image assets. The first, `AppIcon`, is used for the launch icon on the home screen by default. The other one, `sample`, can be used by your code or any widgets in storyboard. You can use the `sample` icon in later exercises.

Note   You can use your favorite image editor to create the images, or download them from `www.pdachoice.com/bookassets`.

Externalize Strings

Generally, you store string texts in external files. Both Android and iOS actually read externalized strings in a similar manner. In Android, the string files are stored in `res/values/strings.xml` in XML format. In iOS, they are stored in "key" = "value"; format in `.strings` files.

To translate the externalized strings from your Android project to an iOS project, do the following:

1. Create a new file anywhere in your Xcode project. For example, to create a new file in "`Supporting Files`" folder first, and do ⌘+N (shortcut key for **New File**).

    a. In the **Choose a template** screen, select **iOS ➤ Resource ➤ Strings File.**

    b. Save as `Localizable.strings`. This is the default file name used by the iOS API.

2. You may copy and comment out the Android counterpart `strings.xml` file into your iOS `Localizable.strings` to start with. Listing 4-1 translates a simple Android `string.xml` to iOS.

Listing 4-1. Translation from Android `strings.xml` to iOS `Localizable.strings`

```
/*
==== copied from HelloAndroid Android project ===
<resources>

  <string name="app_name">HelloAndroid</string>
  <string name="action_settings">Settings</string>
  <string name="hello_world">Hello world!</string>
  <string name="hello_buttn">Hello ...</string>
  <string name="name_hint">Enter a Name, i.e, You</string>

</resources>
*/

"app_name" = "HelloAndroid";
"action_settings" = "Settings";
"hello_world" = "Hello world!";
"hello_buttn" = "Hello ...";
"name_hint" = "Enter a Name, i.e, You";
```

3. To read the strings from the `Localizable.strings` file, use the `NSLocalizedString(...)` method to retrieve the string by key, as shown in Listing 4-2.

Listing 4-2. Read Strings from iOS `Localizable.strings` File

```
// hello_world" = "Hello world!";
var str = NSLocalizedString("hello_world", comment: "")
println(str) // Hello world!
```

With the strings externalized in a text file, you can translate the text to different languages, a common process to implement I18N. Although I am not going to cover Localization/I18N in detail the concept and process actually are the same as in Android.

Common UI Widgets

UI widgets are the interactive software-control components in the application's UI, such as buttons, text fields, and so forth. You create screens to contain the appropriate UI widgets to interact with users, to collect information from users, and/or to display information to users.

The iOS UIKit framework provides rich system UI widgets that you "draw" in storyboard. You also "connect" them to the Swift class as IBOutlet properties so that your code can directly use the view object, update its attributes, or invoke the widget methods to provide dynamic application behaviors.

The rest of this section introduces the common iOS UI widgets and compares them with their Android counterparts. Continuing with the CommonWidgets created previously, do the following:

1. The storyboard already has a storyboard scene that pairs with the ViewController class. This scene won't be tall enough for all the widgets you're going to add. Just to enable you to see all the widgets to be added to this scene, change the Simulated Metrics size to Freeform and make it long enough so you can see all the widgets in storyboard.

2. Select the **View Controller** from storyboard, and in **Size Inspector**, change Simulated Size to Freeform, and make the size 320x1500 (Figure 4-5) to give the view enough height to start with.

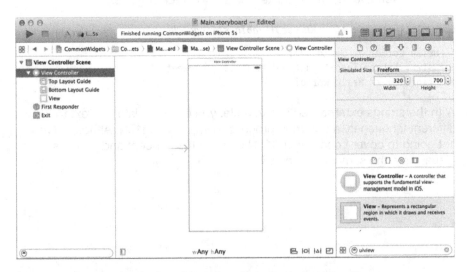

Figure 4-5. Changing the Simulated Metrics size in storyboard to Freeform

Later, you will wrap the whole screen in scroll view in the end so that you can scroll the view up and down.

> **Note**   Don't bother to implement auto layout for each widget in the beginning. The auto layout constraints will get messed up while setting up UIScrollView. Instead, implement the auto layout constraints **after** you set up scroll view.

UILabel

ANDROID ANALOGY
---

android.widget.TextView.

You commonly use UILabel to draw one or multiple lines of static text, such as those that identify other parts of your UI.

Using the Android app as the wireframe, add a UILabel to the iOS CommonWidgets app:

1. Select Main.storyboard, and drag a UILabel from **Object Library** to the root View as shown in Figure 4-6. Drag the widget to position the UILabel as shown in the **Size Inspector**.

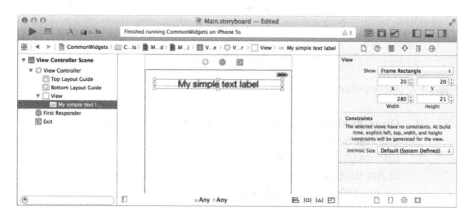

Figure 4-6. Adjusting UILabel size and position

2. Update UILabel attributes in **Attributes Inspector** as shown in Figure 4-7:

   a. Text: **My simple text label**

   b. Alignment: center

   c. The others (**Shadow**, **Autoshrink**, etc.) are all safe to play with, too.

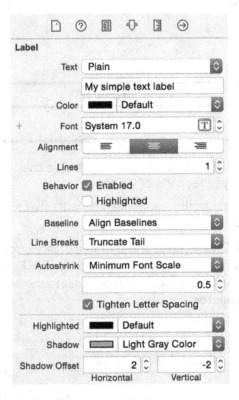

Figure 4-7. Updating UILabel attributes

3. Open **Assistant Editor** and connect the IBOutlet in **Connections Inspector** to your code so that you can update UILabel programmatically. Most of the attributes in **Attributes Inspector** can be modified in the runtime via the IBOutlet mLabel property, as shown in Listing 4-3.

Listing 4-3. UILabel Properties

```
...
@IBOutlet weak var mLabel: UILabel!
override func viewDidLoad() {
  super.viewDidLoad()
  // Do any additional setup after loading the view ...
  self.initLabel()
}

func initLabel() {
  self.mLabel.text = "My simple text label"
  self.mLabel.textColor = UIColor.darkTextColor()
  self.mLabel.textAlignment = NSTextAlignment.Center
  self.mLabel.shadowColor = UIColor.lightGrayColor()
  self.mLabel.shadowOffset = CGSize(width: 2, height: -2)
}
...
```

Build and run the CommonWidgets app to see UILabel live in action (Figure 4-8).

Figure 4-8. A simple iOS UILabel look and feel

UITextField

In iOS, UITextField accepts a single line of user input and shows a placeholder text when the user input is still empty. To learn by example, do the following to use UITextField in the CommonWidgets project.

1. Select Main.storyboard, and drag a UITextField from **Object Library** to the root View as shown in Figure 4-9. Position the UITextField right under the UILabel.

Figure 4-9. *Changing UILabel size and position*

2. Update its attributes in **Attributes Inspector** as shown in Figure 4-10:

   a. Placeholder: **Hint: one-line text input**

   b. Fill in the others as shown in the **Attributes Inspector**.

Figure 4-10. Defining UITextField *in the Attributes Inspector*

3. Open **Assistant Editor** and connect the following
    outlets in **Connections Inspector** to your code as
    shown in Listing 4-4:

    a. Connect IBOutlet to the mTextField property so
        that you can update UITextField programmatically.

    b. Connect the delegate outlet to the ViewController
        class so that the UITextField sends a message to
        its delegate object.

    c. Implement UITextFieldDelegate protocol in
        ViewController. Listing 4-4 shows the common
        way to dismiss the keyboard when the Return key is
        pressed.

Listing 4-4. UITextFieldDelegate

```
class ViewController: UIViewController, UITextFieldDelegate {
  ...
  @IBOutlet weak var mTextField: UITextField!

  // called when 'return' key pressed. return false to ignore.
  func textFieldShouldReturn(textField: UITextField!) -> Bool {
    textField.resignFirstResponder()
    return true
  }
  ...
```

> **Note**   Other methods are defined in UITextFieldDelegate. ⌘-click
> the symbol in editor to bring up the class definition. I normally check the
> method signatures without memorizing them.

Build and run the CommonWidgets app to see UITextField live in action.

UITextView

ANDROID ANALOGY

Multiple-line EditText.

In iOS, UITextView accepts and displays multiple lines of text. To learn by
example, do the following to use UITextView in the CommonWidgets project.

1. Select Main.storyboard, and drag a UITextView from
    Object Library to the root view as shown in Figure 4-11.
    Position the widget right under the UITextField.

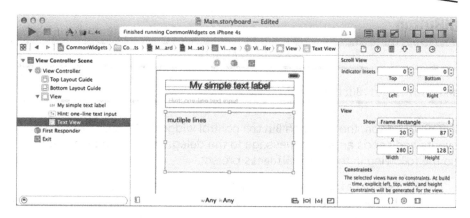

Figure 4-11. *Changing* `UILabel` *size and position*

2. Update its attributes in **Attributes Inspector**:

   a. Text: **multiple lines**

   b. Take a look at its **Attributes Inspector**. Many
      attributes are similar to `UITextField`, but not exact
      (e.g., no `Placeholder`).

3. Open **Assistant Editor** and connect the `IBOutlet` in
   Connections Inspector to your code, `mTextView`, so
   that you can update `UITextView` programmatically. Add
   a method, `logText(...)`, that prints text to `UITextView`.
   You will use it later (see Listing 4-5).

Listing 4-5. `UILabel` *Properties*

```
class ViewController: UIViewController ... {
  ...
  @IBOutlet weak var mTextView: UITextView!
  func logText(text : String) {
    self.mTextView.text = self.mTextView.text + "\n" + text

    // to make sure the last line is visible
    var count = self.mTextView.text.utf16Count // string length
    self.mTextView.scrollRangeToVisible(NSMakeRange(count, 0))
  }
  ...
```

`UITextView` can have multiple lines separated by line breaks. You won't
be able to dismiss the keyboard the same way you normally do for
`UITextField`. Normally, you use another control—for instance, if you have a
save button, you may use it to trigger the `View.resignFirstResponder()` that
dismisses the keyboard.

UIButton

```
ANDROID ANALOGY
```

android.widget.Button.

In iOS, UIButton, the common Button control widget, intercepts touch events and sends an action message to the delegate. To learn by example, do the following in the CommonWidgets project.

1. Select Main.storyboard, drag a UIButton from **Object Library** to the root View, and position the UIButton right under the text view as shown in Figure 4-12.

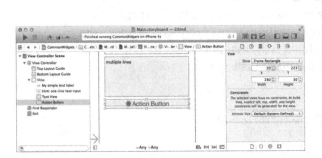

Figure 4-12. UIButton position and attributes

2. Update its attributes in **Attributes Inspector** (see Figure 4-12):

   a. Just like Android Button, most of the Button attributes are associated with the button states. Select the **State Config** first: **Default**

   b. Title: **Action Button**

   c. Image: **sample**

   d. Leave the other attributes as shown in Figure 4-12.

3. Open **Assistant Editor** and connect the IBOutlet and
    IBAction in **Connections Inspector** to your code as
    shown in Listing 4-6.

Listing 4-6. IBOutlet and Implement IBAction

```
class ViewController: UIViewController, UITextFieldDelegate {
  ...
  @IBOutlet weak var mButton: UIButton!
  @IBAction func doButtonTouchDown(sender: AnyObject) {
    println(self.mButton.titleForState(UIControlState.Normal))
    self.mButton.setTitle("Click me!", forState: UIControlState.Normal)
    self.logText("Button clicked")
  }
  ...
```

Build and run the CommonWidgets app to make sure everything is good. When
the button is pressed, it simply logs "Button clicked" text in the UITextView
(See Figure 4-13).

Figure 4-13. Button clicked in UITextView

UISegmentedControl

ANDROID ANALOGY

android.widget.RadioGroup.

In iOS, UISegmentedControl offers closely related but mutually exclusive choices. In Android, RadioGroup offers the same option, but in my opinion, the Android L&F is more of a desktop app or web page style. To show and learn by example, do the following in the CommonWidgets app.

1. Select Main.storyboard, and drag a UISegmentedControl from **Object Library** to the root View under the button as shown in Figure 4-14.

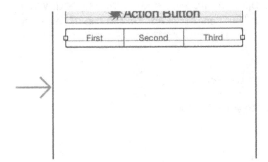 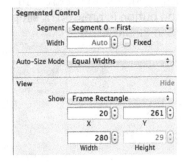

Figure 4-14. UISegmentedControl size and position

2. Update its attribute in **Attributes Inspector** (see Figure 4-15):

    a. Style: **Bar**

    b. Segments: **3**

    c. Title: **First**, **Second**, and **Third** for each segment respectfully.

    d. Optionally, you may assign an **Image** instead of **Title** for each segment.

    e. You may check the **Selected** segment (e.g., **Segment 0**).

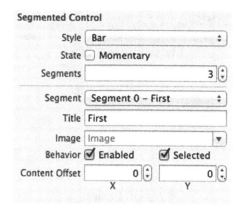

Figure 4-15. UISegmentedControl attributes

3. Open **Assistant Editor** and connect IBOutlet and IBAction in **Connections Inspector** to your code. Frequently, you implement IBAction for the Value Changed events to capture the selections (see Listing 4-7).

Listing 4-7. UISegmentControl IBOutlet and Implement IBAction

```
class ViewController: ...{
  ...
  @IBOutlet weak var mSegmentedControl: UISegmentedControl!
  @IBAction func doScValueChanged(sender: AnyObject) {
    var idx = self.mSegmentedControl.selectedSegmentIndex
    self.logText("segment \(idx)")
  }
  ...
```

Build and run the CommonWidgets app to see how UISegmentedControl in action. Each segment has a zero-based index (see Figure 4-16).

Figure 4-16. UISegmentedControl zero-based index

UISlider

ANDROID ANALOGY

android.widget.SeekBar.

iOS UISlider allows users to make adjustments to a value given a range of allowed values. Users drag the slider left or right to set the value. The interactive nature of the slider makes it a great choice for settings that reflect intensity levels, such as volume, brightness, or color saturation.

To translate the Android SeekBar to the iOS UISlider, do the following:

1. Select Main.storyboard, drag a UISlider from Object Library, and place it below the UISegmentedControl as shown in Figure 4-17.

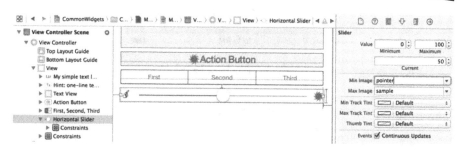

Figure 4-17. Updating the UISlider attributes

2. Update its attribute in **Attributes Inspector** (see Figure 4-17):

    a. Values: min **0** and max **100**

    b. Min and Max **Image**.

    c. Min and Max Track **Tint**.

    d. You may disable **Continuous Updates**.

3. Open **Assistant Editor** and connect IBOutlet and IBAction to your code in **Connections Inspector**. You will often implement IBAction for the Value Changed event to capture the selections (see Listing 4-8).

Listing 4-8. UISlider IBOutlet and implement IBAction

```
class ViewController: ...{
  ...
  @IBOutlet weak var mSlider: UISlider!
  @IBAction func doSliderValueChanged(sender: AnyObject) {
    var value = self.mSlider.value
    self.logText("slider: \(value)")
  }
  ...
}
```

Build and run the CommonWidgets app to see how UISlider in action. As you drag the thumb (the circle on the slider), its value continues to be printed in the UITextView (see Figure 4-18).

Figure 4-18. UISlider value updates

UIActivityIndicatorView

ANDROID ANALOGY

android.widget.ProgressBar default style.

In iOS, UIActivityIndicatorView displays a "busy" activity indicator for a task or something else in progress. This is the so-called indeterminate ProgressBar with a spinning wheel in Android. To port the Android indeterminate ProgressBar to iOS, do the following in the CommonWidgets iOS app:

1. Select Main.storyboard, drag a UIActivityIndicatorView from Object Library, and position it left-aligned and below the UISlider (see Figure 4-19).

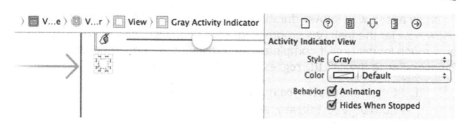

Figure 4-19. UIActivityIndicatorView attributes

2. Update its attribute in **Attributes Inspector** as shown in Figure 4-19:

    a. Style: **Gray**

    b. Color: **Default**

    c. Behavior: both `Animating` and `Hides When Stopped` are commonly enabled.

3. Open **Assistant Editor** and connect IBOutlet in **Connections Inspector** to your code so that you can enable or disable the activity indicator as shown in Listing 4-9.

Listing 4-9. UIActivityIndicatorView IBOutlet

```
class ViewController: ...{
  ...
  @IBOutlet weak var mActivityIndicator: UIActivityIndicatorView!
  func toggleActivityIndicator() {
    var isAnimating = mActivityIndicator.isAnimating()
    isAnimating ? mActivityIndicator.stopAnimating() :
mActivityIndicator.startAnimating()
  }
  ...
```

Build and run the `CommonWidgets` app to see the iOS animated activity indicator. You will call the `toggleActivityIndicator()` method later.

UIProgressView

ANDROID ANALOGY

`android.widget.ProgressBar` horizontal style.

To show a task with known duration in progress, use UIProgressView to show how far the task has progressed. With this, users can better anticipate how much longer until it completes. To translate the Android horizontal ProgressBar to the iOS UIProgressView, do the following:

1. Select Main.storyboard, drag a UIProgressView from Object Library, and position it below and left-aligned to the activity indicator as shown in Figure 4-20.

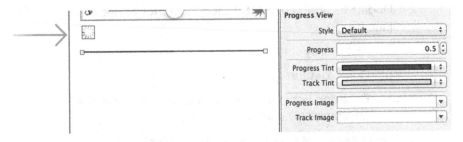

Figure 4-20. UIActivityIndicatorView attributes

2. Update its attributes in **Attributes Inspector** (see Figure 4-20):

    a. Style: **Default (or Bar)**

    b. Progress: **0.5** (between **0.0** and **1.0**)

    c. Progress Tint: **Purple**.

    d. Track Tint: **Yellow**.

3. Open **Assistant Editor** and connect IBOutlet in **Connections Inspector** to your code so that you can update UIProgressView programmatically. Modify the UISlider delegate method, doSliderValueChanged(...) as shown in Listing 4-10, to see the progress change visually (see Figure 4-21).

Listing 4-10. UIActivityIndicatorView IBOutlet

```
class ViewController: ...{
  ...
  @IBAction func doSliderValueChanged(sender: AnyObject) {
    ...
    self.updateProgress(value/100)
  }
```

```
...
@IBOutlet weak var mProgressView: UIProgressView!
func updateProgress(value: Float) {
  self.mProgressView.progress = value
}
...
```

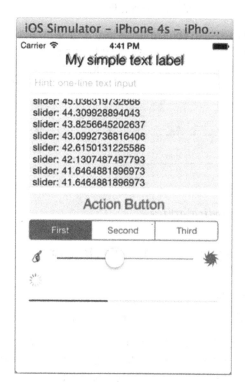

Figure 4-21. UIProgressView update in action

Build and run the CommonWidgets app to visualize iOS UIProgressView in action (see Figure 4-21).

UISwitch

ANDROID ANALOGY

android.widget.Switch, Checkbox, or ToggleButton.

The switch-like widgets are user friendly for presenting mutually exclusive choices. In Android, you may use CheckBox, ToggleButton, or Switch. All are capable for the intended purpose with different L&F.

In iOS, you use UISwitch to allow a user to change values by toggling or dragging the thumb between two states.

To learn UISwitch by example, do the following.

1. Select Main.storyboard and drag a UISwitch from Object Library. Position it to the right of UIActivityIndicatorView (see Figure 4-22).

Figure 4-22. UIActivityIndicatorView

2. Update its attribute in **Attributes Inspector** (see Figure 4-22):

   a. State: **On**

   b. You may change any other attributes safely.

3. Open **Assistant Editor** and connect IBOutlet and IBAction in **Connections Inspector** to your code. You will often implement IBAction for the Value Changed event to capture the selections (see Listing 4-11).

Listing 4-11. UISwitch IBOutlet

```
class ViewController: ...{
  ...
  @IBOutlet var mSwitch: UISwitch!
  @IBAction func doSwitchValueChanged(sender: AnyObject) {
    var isOn = self.mSwitch.on
    self.toggleActivityIndicator()
  }
  ...
```

Build and run the app and toggle the UISwitch to see the activity indicator's animation changes (see Figure 4-23).

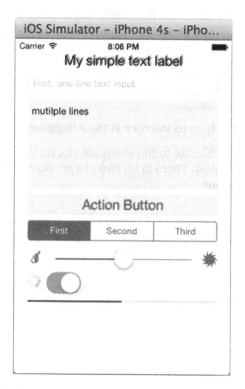

Figure 4-23. *iOS UISwitch look and feel*

UIImageView

android.widget.ImageView.

In iOS, UIImageView displays one image or a series of images for simple graphic animations. For a simple usage like the CommonWidgets app, all you need to do is specify the image source and the attributes in storyboard for how you want to render the image.

To learn iOS `UIImageView` by example, do the following:

1. `UIImageView` can now render vector-based images! This is a new feature in Xcode 6. I only know that the first page of a PDF is rendered nicely. You can definitely use a bitmap image for this exercise, or create a new image set for a PDF file, as shown by the pointers in Figure 4-24:

   a. Select **Images.xcassets** to add a `New Image Set`. Name it `pdf`.

   b. Set the Type to **Vectors** in the **Attributes Inspector**.

   c. Drag a PDF file to the universal slot as shown in Figure 4-24. There is no need to provide 2x or 3x images.

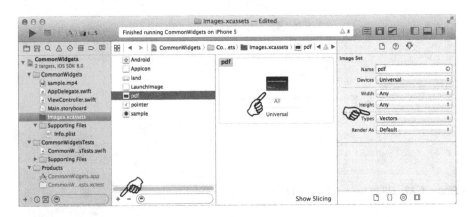

Figure 4-24. create image set

2. Select `Main.storyboard`, drag a `UIImageView` from **Object Library** to the `view`, and position it under the `UIProgressView` as shown in Figure 4-25.

3. Update its attributes in **Attributes Inspector**:

   a. Image: **pdf**

   b. Mode: **Aspect Fit**

   c. Select others as shown in Figure 4-25.

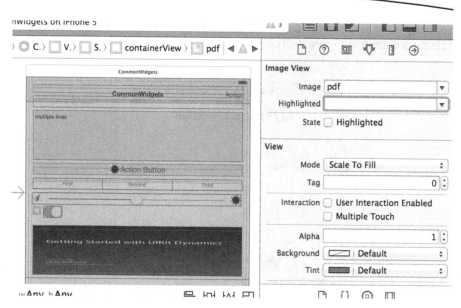

Figure 4-25. UIImageView attributes

4. Open **Assistant Editor** and connect IBOutlet in
   Connections Inspector to your code. Listing 4-12
   demonstrate a simple setImage(...) method that
   assigns an UIImage object to UIImageView.

Listing 4-12. UISwitch IBOutlet

```
class ViewController: ...{
  ...
  @IBOutlet weak var mImageView: UIImageView!
  func setImage(name: String) {
    self.mImageView.image = UIImage(named: name)
  }
  ...
```

As you can see in Figure 4-25, there are very few attributes you would
need to master. However, when it comes down to creating a UIImage and
optimizing size and performance, you want to look into the UIImage class to
see how you would construct the UIImage instances from various sources.
There are actually iOS frameworks that primarily deal with images, like
Quartz 2D or OpenGL. If you know Android OpenGL ES, you definitely want
to take advantage of your existing knowledge and explore the counterpart
iOS OpenGL framework. If you come from a graphics editing background,
Quartz 2D offers a very rich graphics API that will support you for iOS
graphics editing tasks.

You may build and run the `CommonWidgets` iOS app to see `UIImageView` in action as shown in Figure 4-26.

Figure 4-26. `UIImageView` in iPhone 5

Menu

Menu is frequently used to provide quick access to frequently used actions. It is particularly common in desktop and Android platforms. Although there is no such similarly named feature in the iOS SDK, `UIBarButtonItem` in `UIToolbar` or `UINavigationBar` serves a similar purpose as the Android menu system: quick access.

You might also encounter the Android context and popup menus. Again, there is no such menu system in iOS, but I will show you my iOS choices for porting purposes.

UIBarButtonItem

ANDROID ANALOGY

Options Menu or Action Items in ActionBar.

iOS and Android provides widgets for quick access. In iOS, you commonly use UIBarButtonItem in the navigation bar for a limited number of action buttons that can fit into the fixed space. On the iPhone, you may create a bottom bar, UIToolbar, if all of the buttons in UIBarButtonItem don't fit on the navigation bar.

To learn and show the UIBarButtonItem in the navigation bar and toolbar by example, do the following in the CommonWidgets project:

1. Drag a UINavigationBar from **Object Library** to the view and position it on top of the view. Often, it is simpler to add a NavigationController by selecting the **View Controller** in storyboard, and from the Xcode menu bar select **Editor ➤ Embed In ➤ Navigation Controller**. Figure 4-27 depicts the operation results in a new **Navigation Controller** scene and a **Navigation Item** in the existing **View Controller** scene:

   a. Multi-select all the widgets in the scene and reposition them to make room for the top bar.

   b. Update Navigation Item attributes in **Attributes Inspector** (e.g., enter Title: **CommonWidgets**).

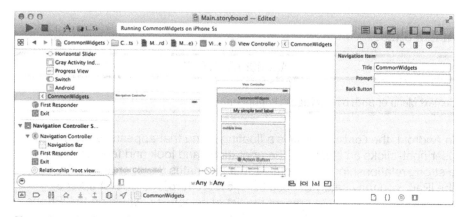

Figure 4-27. Navigation Controller and Navigation Bar

2. Double-click the Navigation Bar to select it, and
    drag-and-drop a `UIBarButtonItem` from the **Object
    Library** on the right side of the **Navigation Bar** to
    add a `rightBarButtonItem` (see Figure 4-28). Choose
    a `Identifier` from selections for those common
    actions. Or enter a title, such as `Action`, as shown
    in Figure 4-28.

Figure 4-28. `UIBarButtonItem` attributes

3. Open **Assistant Editor** and connect the IBAction in the
    `UIBarButtonItem` **Connections Inspector** to your code
    (see Listing 4-13).

Listing 4-13. `UIBarButtonItem` `IBOutlet` and `IBAction`

```
class ViewController: ...{
  ...
  @IBAction func doBarButtonAction(sender: AnyObject) {
    println(">>doBarButtonAction")
  }
  ...
```

Action Sheet

ANDROID ANALOGY

Context Menu or `android.widget.PopupMenu`.

In Android, the `Context Menu` is a floating menu that appears when the
user right-clicks an element. The operations and look and feel establish
a strong relationship to the context that originates the operations. On
the iPad, you may safely choose `UIPopoverController` (see Chapter 3,
`UIPopoverController`) to present the list of selections, which on the iPhone
is automatically presented as full screen.

If you don't want to use full screen, perhaps for a smaller selection, you can also choose UIActionSheet, which is presented as popover for iPad, in an sheet that emerges from the bottom of the screen.

The key SDK class is UIAlertController, which was introduced in Chapter 3 for alert dialogs (see Listing 3-22). To learn the iOS action sheet by example, modify the previous doBarButtonAction(...) IBAction method as shown in Listing 4-14:

1. Create an instance of UIAlertController with the style UIAlertControllerStyle.ActionSheet.

2. You may use Title or Message to establish visual connection to the originating context.

3. It is common to have a destructive UIAlertAction in red for delete or remove, which is specified with the UIAlertActionStyle.Destructive style.

Listing 4-14. UIAlertController with ActionSheet style

```
class ViewController: ...{
...
  @IBAction func doBarButtonAction(sender: AnyObject) {
    println(">>doBarButtonDone: ")

    var actionSheet = UIAlertController(title: "Action (from bar button
item)", message: "Choose an Action", preferredStyle: UIAlertControllerStyle.
ActionSheet)

    // add action buttons
    var actionCancel = UIAlertAction(title: "Cancel", style:
UIAlertActionStyle.Cancel,
        handler: {action in
        // do nothing
        })

    var actionNormal1 = UIAlertAction(title: "Action 1", style:
UIAlertActionStyle.Default,
        handler: {action in
          println(">>actionNormal1")
        })

    var actionNormal2 = UIAlertAction(title: "Action 2", style:
UIAlertActionStyle.Default,
        handler: {action in
          println(">>actionNormal2")
        })
```

```
    var actionDestruct = UIAlertAction(title: "Destruct", style:
UIAlertActionStyle.Destructive,
      handler: {action in
        println(">>actionDestruct")
    })

    actionSheet.addAction(actionCancel) // always the last one
    actionSheet.addAction(actionNormal1)
    actionSheet.addAction(actionNormal2)
    actionSheet.addAction(actionDestruct)

    // UIViewController API to presend viewController
    self.presentViewController(actionSheet, animated: true, completion: nil)
  }
...
```

Build and run the CommonWidgets app to visualize the iOS action sheet
(see Figure 4-29).

Figure 4-29. UIAlertController with ActionSheet style

The android.widget.PopupMenu is anchored to a view. You can do the same thing in iOS by using iOS UIPopoverController to present a UITableViewController. This is either a perfect translation in iPad or a full-screen table view in iPhone. Or, you may use the iOS ActionSheet style to avoid the full-screen UITableView for the iPhone.

UIPickerView

ANDROID ANALOGY

android.widget.Spinner.

In iOS, UIPickerView displays a set of values from which the user selects. It provides a quick way to select one value from a spinning-wheel–like list that shows all or part of the selections.

In traditional desktop apps or web pages, you normally see a drop-down list, or the android.widget.Spinner in Android, for this purpose, except with one trivial difference: they only show the selected value with the other choices folded.

The iOS UIPickerView uses the same pattern as UITableView DataSource to supply the items. To learn by example, add a UIPickerView widget to our CommonWidgets app and do the following:

1. Select Main.storyboard and drag a UIPickerView from **Object Library**. Position it below the UIImageView (see Figure 4-30).

Figure 4-30. Placing the UIPickerView

2. Open **Assistant Editor** and establish `UIPickerView` outlet connections to your code in **Connections Inspector** (see Figure 4-31):

   a. Connect `IBOutlet` to your code.

   b. Connect `delegate` and `dataSource` outlets to `ViewController` class (just like `UITableView` or any widgets using `Data Source`).

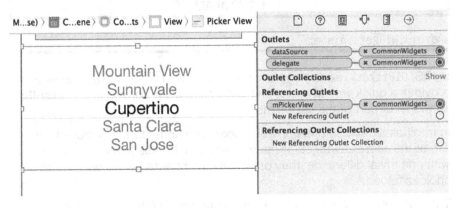

Figure 4-31. Connecting the `UIPickerView` outlets

3. To implement the `UIPickerView` delegate and data source, declare the `ViewController` class to implement `UIPickerViewDelegate` and `UIPickerViewDataSource` protocols as shown in Listing 4-15.

Listing 4-15. `UIPickerView` IBOutlet

```
class ViewController: ..., UIPickerViewDelegate, UIPickerViewDataSource {
  ...
  @IBOutlet weak var mPickerView: UIPickerView!
  // returns the number of 'columns' to display.
  func numberOfComponentsInPickerView(pickerView: UIPickerView) -> Int {
    return 2
  }

  // returns the # of rows in each component..
  func pickerView(pickerView: UIPickerView, numberOfRowsInComponent
component: Int) -> Int {
    return 10
  }
```

```
func pickerView(pickerView: UIPickerView, titleForRow row: Int,
forComponent component: Int) -> String! {
    return "\(component), \(row))"
}

func pickerView(pickerView: UIPickerView, didSelectRow row: Int,
inComponent component: Int) {
    println("\(self.mPickerView.selectedRowInComponent(0))") // before
selection
    println("\(self.mPickerView.selectedRowInComponent(1))")
    println("(\(component), \(row))") // current selection
}
...
```

Build and run the app to see iOS `UIPickerView` in action. The iPhone
emulator is too small for all the widgets you have so far. You need an
Android-like `ScrollView` (which you will implement soon). You can run it in
the iPad emulator for now (see Figure 4-32).

Figure 4-32. UIPickerView in the iPad emulator

Note that if the app looks like a big iPhone while running in the iPad emulator and all the widgets simply scale up, your project deployment info must have been set to **iPhone** only. Change the deployment device to **Universal** under **Deployment Info**, as shown by the pointer in Figure 4-33.

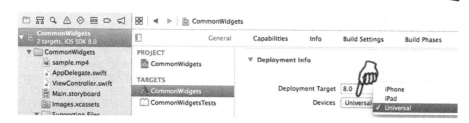

Figure 4-33. *Changing Devices to Universal in Deployment Info*

Play Video

ANDROID ANALOGY

`android.widget.VideoView.`

Similar to Android, the iOS SDK gives you an easy-to-use API to play video resources from a URL. To play full-screen video, you can use the `MPMoviePlayerViewController` class, which already has the appropriate content view and media player controls built in. You only need to present the whole view controller. The following method (see Listing 4-16) demonstrates the simplest usage:

1. Implement the `useMoviePlayerViewController()` method, which plays a video in `MPMoviePlayerViewController` view controller (see Listing 4-16):

   a. Create an instance with a URL. Just like Android, it can link to a remote video source. iOS supports HTTP live-streaming protocol (HLS). You can also create a file URL for bundled content, as shown in the commented code in Listing 4-16. Just as you would in Android, make sure the video format is supported. MPEG4 QuickTime is fairly agnostic, and HLS is good for progressive loading.

   b. `MPMoviePlayerViewController` contains a `MPMoviePlayerController` property, which is the core class to play video. Almost all the customization is done via this property. You will use this class in a moment.

2. Earlier you implemented two actions in an `ActionSheet` (see Figure 4-29). Use the `Action 1` button to trigger the `useMoviePlayerViewController()` method (see Listing 4-16).

Listing 4-16. useMoviePlayerViewController

```
import MediaPlayer
...
class ViewController: ...{
  ...
  @IBAction func doBarButtonAction(sender: AnyObject) {
    ...
    var actionNormal1 = UIAlertAction(title: "Action 1", style:
UIAlertActionStyle.Default,
      handler: {action in
        println(">>actionNormal1")
        self.useMpMoviePlayerViewController()
      })
    ...
  }
  ...
  func useMpMoviePlayerViewController() {
//    var filepath = NSBundle.mainBundle().pathForResource("sample.mp4",
ofType: nil)
//    var fileUrl = NSURL(fileURLWithPath: filepath)
//    var pvc = MPMoviePlayerViewController(contentURL: fileUrl)

    var contentUrl = NSURL(string: "http://devimages.apple.com/iphone/
samples/bipbop/gear3/prog_index.m3u8")
    var pvc = MPMoviePlayerViewController(contentURL: contentUrl)

    pvc.moviePlayer.shouldAutoplay = false;
    pvc.moviePlayer.repeatMode = MPMovieRepeatMode.One

    self.presentViewController(pvc, animated: true, completion: nil)
  }
  ...
```

3. To play video in non-fullscreen mode, use the
    MPMoviePlayerController directly to play video in a
    View widget:

    a. Select Main.storyboard, drag a UIView from **Object
        Library**, and position it below the UIPickerView as
        shown in Figure 4-34. This is the viewing area that
        shows the video.

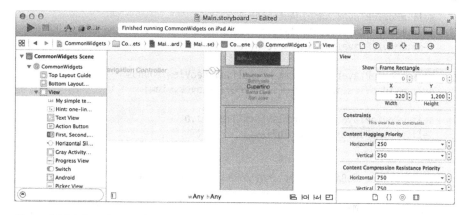

Figure 4-34. *View element for the video*

b. Open the **Assistant Editor** to Connect IBOutlet in **Connections Inspector** to your code, mVideoView property.

c. Create a stored property for the MPMoviePlayerController instance to allow users to seek through, play, or stop the playback.

d. In viewDidLoad(...), invoke the useMoviePlayerController() method to prepare the video to play.

e. Use the Action 2 button to start the video. (see Listing 4-17).

Listing 4-17. Using the MPMoviePlayercontroller

```
class ViewController: ...{
  ...
  override func viewDidLoad() {
    ...
    self.useMoviePlayerController()
  }
  ...
  @IBOutlet weak var mVideoView: UIView!
  var mMoviePlayer : MPMoviePlayerController!
  func useMoviePlayerController() {
    var url = NSURL(string:
"http://devimages.apple.com/iphone/samples/bipbop/gear3/prog_index.m3u8")
    self.mMoviePlayer = MPMoviePlayerController(contentURL: url)
```

```
  self.mMoviePlayer.shouldAutoplay = false
  self.mMoviePlayer.controlStyle = MPMovieControlStyle.Embedded
  self.mMoviePlayer.setFullscreen(false, animated: true)

  self.mMoviePlayer.view.frame = self.mVideoView.bounds
  self.mVideoView.addSubview(self.mMoviePlayer.view)

  self.mMoviePlayer.currentPlaybackTime = 2.0
  self.mMoviePlayer.prepareToPlay()
}
...
@IBAction func doBarButtonAction(sender: AnyObject) {
  ...
  var actionNormal2 = UIAlertAction(title: "Action 2", style:
UIAlertActionStyle.Default,
    handler: {action in
      self.mMoviePlayer.play()
    })
  ...
}
```

Build and run the app. Select Action 1 for full screen and Action 2 to play video embedded in a subview. You don't have the Android-like ScrollView yet, but you can run it in the iPad emulator for now (see Figure 4-35).

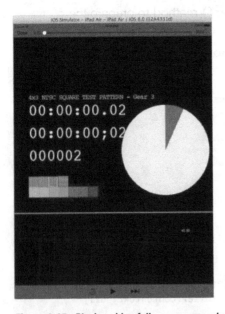

Figure 4-35. Playing video full screen vs. embedded in the iPad emulator

WebView

ANDROID ANALOGY

`android.widget.WebView.`

You can display rich HTML content in your mobile apps on almost all the popular mobile platforms, including iOS, Android, BlackBerry, and Windows phones. This enables you to deliver web content as part of your mobile apps. One common scenario is when you want to provide information in your app that needs to be updated frequently, and you want to host the content online as a web page. To take it one step further, the web content does not have to be remote; you can bundle the web page content with the native app. This enables web developers to leverage their web development skills and create so-called hybrid apps.

With new features from HTML5 and CSS3, many web developers are creating meaningful and interactive web apps that are shortening the gap between native apps and mobile web apps. In iOS, the key SDK class is `UIWebView`, and it does support many HTML5 and CSS3 features (e.g., `Offline Cache` and `WebSocket`, etc.).

As an example, the following steps demonstrate common tasks using `UIWebView`:

1. Select `Main.storyboard`, drag a `UIWebView` from the **Object Library**, and position it below the video `View` (see Figure 4-36). Set its attributes in **Attributes Inspector**; it is commonly set **Scales Page To Fit**.

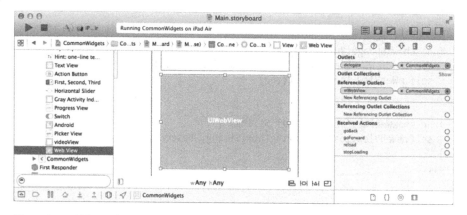

Figure 4-36. *iOS* `UIWebView` *attributes in the Connections Inspector*

2. As usual, open **Assistant Editor** and connect the following outlets in **Connections Inspector** to your code (see Figure 4-36):

   a. Connect IBOutlet so you can use the widget in your code.

   b. Connect the delegate outlet so your code can intercept UIWebView life-cycle events.

3. Listing 4-18 demonstrates the programming code commonly used for UIWebView.

   a. Use loadRequest(...) to load the URL. You can also create a file URL to load a local HTML file.

   b. Use loadHTMLString(...) to render simple string text.

   c. Although not demonstrated here, you can also use loadData(...) to render NSData that you normally get from remote contents using NSURLConnection, which I will demonstrate later in the "NSURLConnection" section.

Listing 4-18. UIWebView Code for Loading a URL or String Text

```
class ViewController: ... {
  ...
  override func viewDidLoad() {
    ...
//    self.showWebPage(url: "http://pdachoice.com/me/webview")
    self.showWebPage(htmlString: "<H1>Hello UIWebView</H1>")
  }
  ...
  @IBOutlet weak var mWebView: UIWebView!
  func showWebPage(#url: String) {
    var req = NSURLRequest(URL: NSURL(string: url)!)
    self.mWebView.loadRequest(req)
  }

  func showWebPage(#htmlString: String) {
    self.mWebView.loadHTMLString(htmlString, baseURL: nil)
  }
  ...
```

4. To intercept UIWebView life-cycle events, implement
    the UIWebViewDelegate protocol as shown in
    Listing 4-19.

Listing 4-19. UIWebViewDelegate protocol

```
class ViewController: ... , UIWebViewDelegate{
  ...
  func webView(webView: UIWebView, shouldStartLoadWithRequest request:
NSURLRequest, navigationType: UIWebViewNavigationType) -> Bool {
    // do something, like re-direct or intercept etc.
    return true; // false to stop http request
  }
  func webViewDidStartLoad(webView: UIWebView) {
    // do something, e.g., start UIActivityViewIndicator
    self.mActivityIndicator.startAnimating()
  }
  func webViewDidFinishLoad(webView: UIWebView) {
    // do something, e.g., stop  UIActivityViewIndicator
    self.mActivityIndicator.stopAnimating()
  }
  func webView(webView: UIWebView, didFailLoadWithError error: NSError) {
    // do something, i.e., show error alert
    self.mActivityIndicator.stopAnimating()
    var alert = UIAlertController(title: "Error", message:
error.localizedDescription, preferredStyle: UIAlertControllerStyle.Alert)
    alert.addAction(UIAlertAction(title: "Close", style: UIAlertActionStyle.
Cancel, handler: nil))
    self.presentViewController(alert, animated: true, completion: nil)
  }
  ...
```

Build and run the app to see iOS UIWebView in action. Now, even the iPad Air
screen is too small (see Figure 4-37). You need an Android-like ScrollView,
which you will implement next.

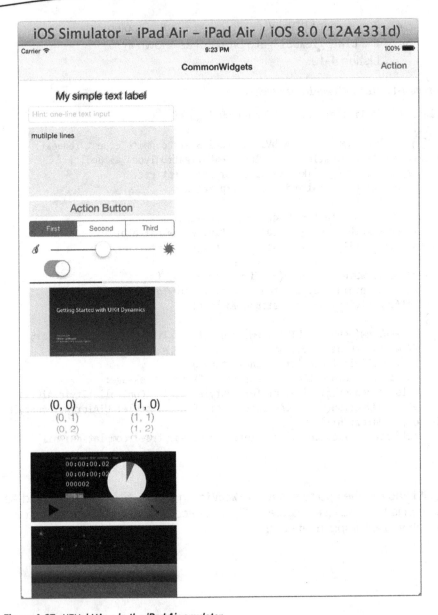

Figure 4-37. UIWebView in the iPad Air emulator

ScrollView

ANDROID ANALOGY
---

android.widget.ScrollView.

Due to the smaller screen size on mobile devices, ScrollView is very useful for displaying a content view larger than the physical display. To implement this in iOS, you use UIScrollView.

To make UIScrollView work with auto layout, it is easier to wrap all the widgets in a container view first, which will let you lay out the widgets in the container view as you normally would with auto layout.

The following steps demonstrate how you would normally do this with iOS UIScrollView in the CommonWidgets app:

1. Select all widgets in the root View, select
   Embed In ➤ View from the Xcode menu bar
   to embed all these common widgets in a View
   (see Figure 4-38), and change this storyboard label
   to containerView.

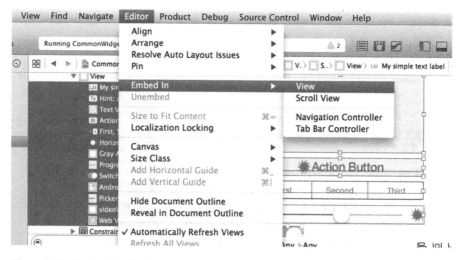

Figure 4-38. Embed all widgets in a View

2. Change **View Controller Simulated Size** to **Fixed**.
   The storyboard scene becomes shorter, with
   some widgets left out of the screen as shown in
   Figure 4-39.

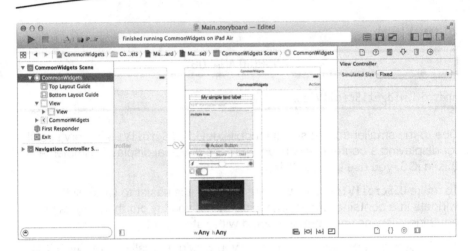

Figure 4-39. Change scene to Fixed size

3. With the container, you can scroll the `containerView` as a whole by embedding the `containerView` in `UIScrollView`. Select containerView first and embed it in a scroll view as shown in Figure 4-40 (**Menubar ➤ Editor ➤ Embed In ➤ Scroll View**).

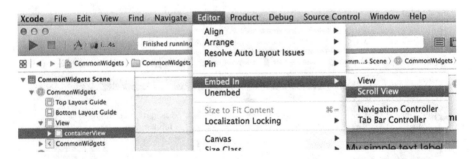

Figure 4-40. Embed `containerView` in a scroll view

4. Open the **Add New Constraints** popup and pin the `UIScrollView` edges to the edge of the super view with zero spacing, and update the Frame (see Figure 4-41).

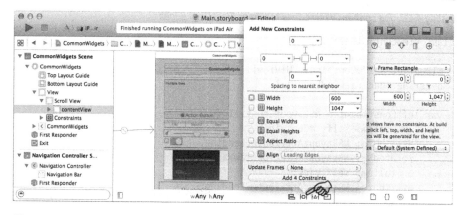

Figure 4-41. Set the UIScrollView position

5. The preceding operation shifts the contentView. In contentView **Size Inspector**, reposition the contentView at (0,0) with size 600 (do **not** change the height).

6. The auto layout constraints are repurposed for calculating the scrolling position. You have to create auto layout constraints to pin the edges to the parent UIScrollView with zero spacing (see Figure 4-42).

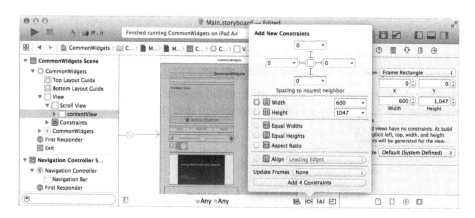

Figure 4-42. contentView pinned to UIScrollView with zero spacing

7. To makes the containerView adaptive to size classes, create constraints that align the widget to the parent's leading and trailing edges. Currently, you cannot use storyboard to draw auto layout for this, so you have to write code as shown in Listing 4-20.

Listing 4-20. Pin contentView Edges to Screen/Root View Edges

```
class ViewController: ... {
  ...
  @IBOutlet var mContainer: UIView!
  override func viewDidLoad() {
  ...
  var leftConstraint = NSLayoutConstraint(
          item: self. mContainer,
      attribute: NSLayoutAttribute.Leading,
      relatedBy: NSLayoutRelation(rawValue: 0)!,
         toItem: self.view,
      attribute: NSLayoutAttribute.Leading,
     multiplier: 1.0,
       constant: 0)
   self.view.addConstraint(leftConstraint)

  var rightConstraint = NSLayoutConstraint(
          item: self. mContainer,
      attribute: NSLayoutAttribute.Trailing,
      relatedBy: NSLayoutRelation(rawValue: 0)!,
         toItem: self.view,
      attribute: NSLayoutAttribute.Trailing,
     multiplier: 1.0,
       constant: 0)
   self.view.addConstraint(rightConstraint)

  }
  ...
```

8. You can also set the other widgets for auto layout so they adapt to different size classes.

Build and run the app to see iOS UIScrollView in action. You should be able to see all the widgets by scrolling the view up and down (see Figure 4-43).

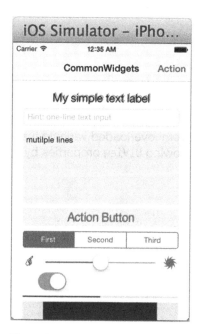
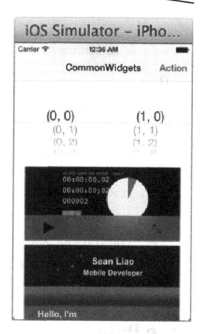

Figure 4-43. CommonWidgets with scrollable view

Animations

Back in the old days, I cared a lot less about animation effects, but I think the evolution of iOS definitely raised the bar. In iOS, you can animate UIView properties using the simple UIView animation API.

To learn by example, modify the existing UISegmentedControl.doScValueChanged(...) method as shown in Listing 4-21 to create some animation effects using the UIView.animateWithDuration(...) method.

Listing 4-21. UIView.animateWithDuration(...)

```
...
@IBAction func doScValueChanged(sender: AnyObject) {
  var idx = self.mSegmentedControl.selectedSegmentIndex
  self.logText("segment \(idx)")
  let center = self.mButton.center
  UIView.animateWithDuration(1, animations: { action in
    self.mButton.center = CGPoint(x: center.x, y: center.y / (idx + 1))
    self.mButton.alpha = 1 / (idx + 1)
    }, completion: { action in
      UIView.animateWithDuration(1, delay: 0, usingSpringWithDamping: 0.5,
initialSpringVelocity: 0.5, options: UIViewAnimationOptions.CurveEaseInOut,
animations: { action in
```

```
          self.mButton.center = center
        }, completion: {   action in
          // do nothing
        })
    })
}
...
```

The `UIView.animateWithDuration(...)` has several overloaded variants that all work the same way. You can animate the following `UIView` properties by modifying them inside the animation block:

- frame for the viewing area,

- center for position,

- transform for scale and rotation,

- alpha for transparency, and

- backgroundColor.

Save Data

Saving data is an essential programming task in almost all common programming platforms. In addition to transactional data, most of the mobile apps also save application states and user preferences so that users can resume their tasks later. Both iOS and Android provide several persistent storage options. The iOS SDK offers the following choices:

- User Defaults System storage

- File storage

- CoreData framework and SQLite database (not covered in this book)

Before diving into the first two options, you will create an Xcode project so that you can write code and visualize how these options work.

1. Launch Xcode, use the **Single View Application** template, and name the project SaveData.

2. Create a Navigation Bar with an `UIBarButtonItem` (see Figure 4-44):

   a. Select the **View Controller** in storyboard, and from the Xcode menu bar, select **Editor ➤ Embed In ➤ Navigation Controller**.

   b. In the Navigation Item **Attributes Inspector**, enter a Title of **SaveData**.

c. Drag a `BarButtonItem` from **Object Library** and drop it onto the Navigation Item in the **View Controller** scene. Update the Bar Item `Title` in **Attributes Inspector** to be **Delete**.

d. Select the `Bar Button Item` and open **Assistant Editor** to connect the selector outlet to your code. Name the `IBAction` **doDelete**.

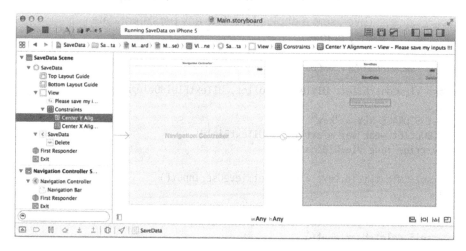

Figure 4-44. *SaveData project storyboard*

3. Create a `UITextField` to get user input as shown in Figure 4-44:

a. Drag a `UITextField` onto the **View Controller** scene. In the **Attributes Inspector**, enter the placeholder, `"Please save my inputs !!!"`.

b. Add auto layout constraints to center the `UITextField` in the `View`.

4. Open **Assistant Editor**, and in the `UITextField` **Connections Inspector** connect the following outlets to your code:

a. Connect `Referencing Outlet` to `IBOutlet` property, `mTextField`.

b. Connect `delegate` to your `ViewController` class.

5.   Implement `UITextFieldDelegate` protocol in the
`ViewController` class and create the stubs that will
triggers the retrieve, save, and delete code as shown in
Listing 4-22:

a.   Load the saved data in
`ViewController.viewDidLoad()`.

b.   Save the user input when the Return key is pressed.

c.   Give users a choice to delete any persistent data
they created.

Listing 4-22. SaveData ViewController

```
class ViewController: UIViewController, UITextFieldDelegate {
  ...
  let STORAGE_KEY = "key"
  @IBOutlet weak var mTextField: UITextField!
  override func viewDidLoad() {
    ...
    self.mTextField.text = self.retrieveUserInput()
  }

  @IBAction func doDelete(sender: AnyObject) {
    self.deleteUserInput();
  }

  func textFieldShouldReturn(textField: UITextField!) -> Bool {
    ...
    self.saveUserInput(self.mTextField.text)
    return true
  }

  func saveUserInput(str: String) {
    // TODO
  }

  func retrieveUserInput() -> String? {
    // TODO
    return nil
  }

  func deleteUserInput() {
    // TODO
  }
  ...
```

Nothing is new yet. Build and run the SaveData project (see Figure 4-45).

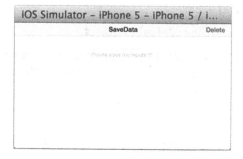

Figure 4-45. The SaveData project display

Without completing the method stubs, this new project exhibits a common problem that can be observed in the following three steps:

1. Enter something in the input text field.

2. Exit the app.

3. Relaunch the app. The previous input is gone!

For typical app settings or user preferences, users are not happy if they need to reenter them every time they launch the app. The app needs to save the data and load it back when the app restarts.

NSUserDefaults

ANDROID ANALOGY

SharedPreferences.

Just like Android's SharedPreferences, which saves key-value pairs of primitive data types, you use NSUserDefaults class to interface with iOS's User Defaults system for the same purpose. NSUserDefaults takes care of data caching and syncing for developers. It is easy to use and its performance is already optimized.

The values to be managed in the iOS defaults system can be primitives or the so-called property list object (e.g., NSData, NSString, NSNumber, NSDate, NSArray, or NSDictionary). For NSArray and NSDictionary objects, their contents must be property list objects as well.

Continue with the SaveData project. You are going to fix the problem you just observed.

1. Create the convenient methods that save, retrieve, and delete data using the NSUserDefaults API (see Listing 4-23):

    a. Get the NSUserDefaults object.

    b. You may accumulate multiple updates and call synchronize() to send the batched updates to the defaults system storage.

Listing 4-23. Save, Retrieve, and Delete in defaults system

```
class ViewController: UIViewController, UITextFieldDelegate {
  ...
  let userDefaults = NSUserDefaults.standardUserDefaults()
  func saveUserdefault(data: AnyObject, forKey: String) {
    userDefaults.setObject(data, forKey: forKey)
    userDefaults.synchronize()
  }

  func retrieveUserdefault(key: String) -> String? {
    var obj = userDefaults.stringForKey(key)
    return obj
  }

  func deleteUserDefault(key: String) {
    self.userDefaults.removeObjectForKey(key)
  }
  ...
```

2. Earlier, you already created the stubs that are wired to the right events. Call the convenient methods just created to complete the persistent code (see Listing 4-24).

Listing 4-24. Save, Retrieve, and Delete using the UserDefaults system

```
class ViewController: UIViewController, UITextFieldDelegate {
  ...
  func saveUserInput(str: String) {
    self.saveUserdefault(str, forKey: STORAGE_KEY)
  }

  func retrieveUserInput() -> String? {
    return self.retrieveUserdefault(STORAGE_KEY)
  }
```

```
func deleteUserInput() {
  self.deleteUserDefault(STORAGE_KEY)
}
...
```

Relaunch the SaveData project and repeat the failed test case. You should no longer need to reenter the name when reopening the app.

File Storage

Just like Java, the iOS SDK provides system APIs to interface with the file system. In iOS, you commonly use the following API:

- The NSFileManager class.

- The NSString, NSArray, NSDictionary, and NSData Foundation classes also have convenient methods to store and retrieve themselves from file systems.

NSFileManager

If you need to perform any file-related tasks to manipulate File and Directory, the NSFileManager class provides the API to do the work. You need to specify the file path or file URL for the destination file and specify the NSData object for the file contents.

To show and to learn by example, use NSFileManager to achieve the same save/retrieve/delete purpose.

1. Create the convenient methods that save, retrieve, and delete data using the NSFileManager API (see Listing 4-25):

    a. Get the NSFileManager object.

    b. Use NSHomeDirectory(). stringByAppendingPathComponent(...) to build the iOS file path.

c. NSFileManager deals with NSData, which can be converted to common Foundation data types (e.g., String, array and dictionary).

Listing 4-25 . Manage Data in files using NSFileManager

```
class ViewController: UIViewController, UITextFieldDelegate {
  ...
  let fileMgr = NSFileManager.defaultManager()
  func saveToFile(str: String, file: String) {
    var path = NSHomeDirectory().stringByAppendingPathComponent("Documents").
stringByAppendingPathComponent(file)
    var data = str.dataUsingEncoding(NSUTF8StringEncoding)
    var ok = fileMgr.createFileAtPath(path, contents: data, attributes: nil)
  }

  func retrieveFromFile(file: String) -> String? {
    var path = NSHomeDirectory().stringByAppendingPathComponent("Documents").
stringByAppendingPathComponent(file)
    var data = fileMgr.contentsAtPath(path)
    var str = NSString(data:data, encoding: NSUTF8StringEncoding)

    return str
  }

  func deleteFile(file: String) {
    var path = NSHomeDirectory().stringByAppendingPathComponent("Documents").
stringByAppendingPathComponent(file)
    var ok = fileMgr.removeItemAtPath(path, error: nil)
  }
  ...
```

> **Note**   Each app can only write to certain folders inside the application home (e.g., the Documents folder). As in Android, the most common write error is probably trying to create a file in the wrong place.

2. Call the convenient methods just created to complete the persistent code that uses NSFileManager (see Listing 4-26).

Listing 4-26. Save, Retrieve, and Delete in File using NSFileManager

```
class ViewController: UIViewController, UITextFieldDelegate {
  ...
  func saveUserInput(str: String) {
//    self.saveUserdefault(str, forKey: STORAGE_KEY)
    self.saveToFile(str, file: STORAGE_KEY)
  }

  func retrieveUserInput() -> String? {
//    return self.retrieveUserdefault(STORAGE_KEY)
    return self.retrieveFromFile(STORAGE_KEY)
  }

  func deleteUserInput() {
//    self.deleteUserDefault(STORAGE_KEY)
    self.deleteFile(STORAGE_KEY)
  }
  ...
```

Many Foundation data types contains convenient methods to interface with
File for saving and retrieving themselves. Listing 4-27 depicts the code that
saves and retrieves the string itself:

Listing 4-27. Save String using Foundation Class API

```
  func saveToFile(str: String, file: String) {
    var path = ...
    var error: NSError?
    str.writeToFile(path, atomically: true, encoding: NSUTF8StringEncoding,
error: &error)
  }

  func retrieveFromFile(file: String) -> String? {
    var path = ...
    var error: NSError?
    var str = String(contentsOfFile: path, encoding:
NSUTF8StringEncoding, error: &error)

    return str
  }
```

You can find the same writeToFile(...) and constructor(...) methods in NSDictionary, NSArray, and NSData for saving and retrieve themselves as well. Just for a quick exercise, Listing 4-28 serves the same purpose as Listing 4-27:

Listing 4-28. Save String using Foundation Class API instead of using the NSFileManager API

```
let KEY_JSON = "aKey"
func saveJsonToFile(str: String, file: String) {
  var path = ...
  // one entry dict, for sure can have more
  var ser = NSDictionary(objects: [str], forKeys: [KEY_JSON])
  ser.writeToFile(path, atomically: true)
}

func retrieveJsonFromFile(file: String) -> String? {
  var path = ...
  var ser = NSDictionary(contentsOfFile: path)!
  return ser[KEY_JSON] as String?
}
```

This is particularly useful when dealing with JSON messages because most remote messages are in JSON format nowadays.

Generally, you only need to use NSFileManager directly for pure file-system operations like inspecting file attributes, or iterating thru files in directories.

Networking and Using Remote Service

A typical client-server solution hosts information on the server side, while client apps either fetch data from the server and present it to users in meaningful ways, or collect data from the users to submit to the server. You probably hear the buzzwords "mobile commerce" or "m-commerce" a lot nowadays. To describe them in simple terms, mobile apps fetch product items from a server and then submit the purchase orders to the server via the Internet. From a mobile-apps programming perspective, this is really not new at all. It is still a client-server programming topic using HTTP GET/POST, which is what most of the e-commerce web sites do.

I will talk about JSON messages and RESTful services for mobile apps specifically because of their popularity versus traditional SOAP-based web services.

Perform Network Operations in Background

For apps with a user interface, you want to perform I/O tasks or network-related code in the background, and do UI updates in the UI main thread. Otherwise, the app appears to the user to lag because the UI thread is blocked, waiting for the task to finish. This principle applies to iOS, Android, and probably any UI platforms. The Android SDK provides the convenient android.os.AsyncTask class to perform tasks in a background thread and hook back to the UI main thread when the background task is completed. Generally, when interfacing with a remote server, you want to fetch data in the background thread. When the remote data is received, your UI code presents the data on the screen.

To show how to achieve the same objectives in iOS, you will create a simple iOS app, as shown in Figure 4-46, to demonstrate some basic RESTFul client code that consumes remote RESTFul services:

- When the GET or POST button is selected, the app sends HTTP GET or POST to the server in a background thread.

- When the HTTP response is received, the app renders the data on the user interface.

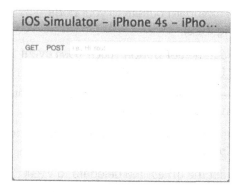

Figure 4-46. The iOS RestClient app

Create a new Xcode project to have a fresh start.

1. Launch Xcode, use the **Single View Application** template, and name the project RestClient.

2. Draw your storyboard with the following widgets (see Figure 4-47):

   a. A UIButton to invoke HTTP GET

   b. A UIButton to invoke HTTP POST

   c. A UITextField to take user input

   d. A UIWebView to render the HTTP response

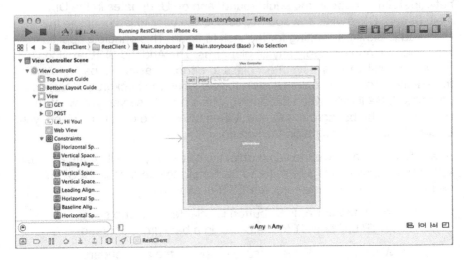

Figure 4-47. RestClient storyboard

3. Connect storyboard outlets to your code
    (see Listing 4-29):

    a. Connect the GET button Touch Down event to your
        doGet()IBAction method.

    b. Connect the POST button Touch Down event to your
        doPost()IBAction method.

    c. Connect the UITextField delegate outlet to
        ViewController class.

    d. Connect the UIWebView delegate to ViewController
        class.

    e. Connect the text field New Referencing Outlet to
        the ViewController mTextField IBOutlet property

    f. Connect the webview New Referencing Outlet to
        the ViewController mWebView IBOutlet property

Listing 4-29. RestClient Preparation Code

```
class ViewController: UIViewController, UITextFieldDelegate,
UIWebViewDelegate {

  @IBOutlet weak var mWebView: UIWebView!
  @IBOutlet weak var mTextField: UITextField!

  override func viewDidLoad() {
    super.viewDidLoad()
    // Do any additional setup after loading the view ...
  }

  func textFieldShouldReturn(textField: UITextField!) -> Bool {
    textField.resignFirstResponder();
    return true
  }

  @IBAction func doGet(sender: AnyObject) {
  }

  @IBAction func doPost(sender: AnyObject) {
  }
}
```

Nothing is new yet, just the repeated storyboard tasks and the process of connecting the outlets to your code with the method stubs. You will fill the main topics in these stubs next.

RESTFul Service using HTTP

Most of the RESTFul services support HTTP/HTTPS protocols. Since the RESTFul services are supposed to be agnostic to client apps, it is not surprising that your Android code most likely can be translated nicely to the iOS platform if it consumes the same RESTFul services. To retrieve data from most RESTFul services, it is similar to how browsers use HTTP GET to fetch a remote HTML file. You can use HTTP GET to fetch an HTML document from mobile apps, too—or it can fetch any data, such as raw bytes, an XML or JSON document, and so forth.

To submit user input, you will very often use HTML Form to submit form data from an HTML page to HTTP servers. The form data is transmitted using the HTTP POST method. This is very common in iOS and Android apps as well. Technically speaking, you can also send a query string to an HTTP server using the HTTP GET method, just as some web pages do. In this case, you can simply build the URL with query strings and use the HTTP

GET method to send data to your server. It is a design decision that you will make by understanding usages and conventions of GET versus POST. The key is to design the interface so both your mobile clients and the server can understand it.

NSURLConnection

```
ANDROID ANALOGY
```

HttpURLConnection.

To interface with HTTP protocol in iOS, you can use the NSURLConnection class to send GET and POST URL requests. The API is fairly similar to Android's HttpUrlConnection.

Continue with the RestClient project and add code to send HTTP requests by doing the following:

1. Implement the IBAction doGet() method to send the HTTP GET request and to get data from the HTTP response (see Listing 4-30):

    a. Create an NSMutableURLRequest object.

> **Note**   You commonly escape/encode the URL path or query string just like you normally do using URLEncoder in Android.

    b. Set HTTP method to GET.

> **Note**   An HTTP method is case-sensitive according to HTTP protocol specs.

    c. Set the accept header, which is commonly used for content negotiation (e.g., text/html, json/application, etc.).

> **Note**   Our sample echo service supports "text/html", "text/
> plain", and "application/json" content types. To demonstrate
> the content negotiation visually, I choose to use a UIWebView widget to
> render the server response and specify the "text/html". In general,
> "application/json" is more suitable for data exchange.

    d. NSURLConnection.sendAsynchronousRequest sends
        asynchronous HTTP Request and receives the HTTP
        response in the completionHandler closure in the UI
        main thread.

Listing 4-30. HTTP GET

```
let URL_TEST = "http://pdachoice.com/ras/service/echo/"
@IBAction func doGet(sender: AnyObject) {
  var text = self.mTextField.text.
stringByAddingPercentEncodingWithAllowedCharacters(NSCharacterSet.
URLPathAllowedCharacterSet())
  var url = URL_TEST + text
  var urlRequest = NSMutableURLRequest(URL: NSURL(string: url)!)
    urlRequest.HTTPMethod = "GET"
    urlRequest.setValue("text/html", forHTTPHeaderField: "accept")

  NSURLConnection.sendAsynchronousRequest(urlRequest, queue:
NSOperationQueue.mainQueue(),
    completionHandler: {(resp: NSURLResponse!, data: NSData!, error:
NSError!) -> Void in
      self.mWebView.loadData(data, MIMEType: resp.MIMEType,
textEncodingName: resp.textEncodingName, baseURL: nil)
    })
  }
```

    2.   Implement the IBAction doPost() method to send
         HTTP POST to post data to the server and receive an
         HTTP response (see Listing 4-31). Almost the same
         as sending HTTP GET, you use NSURLConnection.
         sendAsynchronousRequest to send asynchronous
         HTTP messages, except you set the HTTP method
         to POST:

        a. Make sure set the HTTP method is set to POST.

        b. POST data has the same format as a query string,
           but you want to encode it to put in the HTTP Body,
           the same way you do in Android.

c. To parse JSON content or create a JSON object,
   NSJSONSerialization is your friend. You want to
   convert the JSON object to NSDictionary or the
   JSON array to NSArray.

Listing 4-31. HTTP POST

```
@IBAction func doPost(sender: AnyObject) {
  var text = self.mTextField.text.
stringByAddingPercentEncodingWithAllowedCharacters(
      NSCharacterSet.URLQueryAllowedCharacterSet())
  var queryString = "echo=" + text;
  var formData = queryString.dataUsingEncoding(NSUTF8StringEncoding)!
  var urlRequest = NSMutableURLRequest(URL: NSURL(string: URL_TEST)!)
  urlRequest.HTTPMethod = "POST"
  urlRequest.HTTPBody = formData

  urlRequest.setValue("application/json", forHTTPHeaderField: "accept")

  NSURLConnection.sendAsynchronousRequest(urlRequest,
    queue: NSOperationQueue.mainQueue(),
    completionHandler: {(resp: NSURLResponse!, data: NSData!, error:
NSError!) -> Void in
      println(resp.MIMEType)
      println(NSString(data: data, encoding: NSUTF8StringEncoding))

      var json = NSJSONSerialization.JSONObjectWithData(data, options:
        NSJSONReadingOptions.AllowFragments, error: nil) as NSDictionary
      self.mWebView.loadHTMLString(json["echo"] as String, baseURL: nil)
    })
})
}
```

> **Note** SERVER_URL = "http://pdachoice.com/ras/service/echo" is
> a simple web service that echoes back the path parameter. Desktop browsers
> are fully capable of rendering plain text as well as HTML documents. You can
> use a desktop browser to verify the data from the server.

Build and run the RestClient project and enter **"Hi you!"** to see the live app
in action. The simple echo service with the GET method actually responded
in HTML format, <html><body><h1>Hi you!</h1></body></html>, which is
rendered as shown in Figure 4-48.

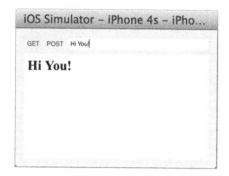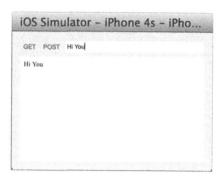

Figure 4-48. RestClient doGet and doPost responses

Summary

This chapter introduced the most common programming component mappings from Android to iOS:

- User interface and UI widgets
- Persistent storage options
- Network and remote services with JSON

Many meaningful apps only ever deal with the components discussed herein. This chapter listed all the viable mappings with step-by-step instructions on how to translate Android components to their iOS counterparts. You will see how to apply these guidelines to build a simple but complete utility app from start to finish next.

Part III

Pulling It All Together

Previously, you have covered many discrete Android-to-iOS mapping topics. They are purposely self-contained with very few classes in the individual Xcode projects so they can serve as independent sample projects. In the real programming world, it is the combination of features and use cases that makes your app useful and entertaining. You will definitely need to apply more than one mapping guideline to complete a meaningful app.

To walk you through the whole porting process, you will port a fully functioning Android app from start to finish by applying the mapping topics from Part II:

1. Create the runnable storyboard using the counterpart live Android app as the wireframe.

2. Port the Android classes and classes' member signatures to Swift first. Preserve any signatures if possible.

3. Fill in the blanks one method at a time. The caller, receivers, and "dots" mostly will just connect to each other without any glitch by blindly translating the Java statements or expressions to Swift at the method level.

Nothing will really be new here; you will systematically repeat the same top-down development approach you have been taking, and implement one piece at a time.

Chapter 5

Recap with a Case Study

Thus far in this book, you have covered many discrete Android-to-iOS mapping topics and created more than 10 Xcode projects. Those mapping topics were purposely implemented in individual Xcode projects with very few classes. In Chapter 3, you learned the top-down development approach using the storyboard to break the whole app into MVC-oriented content view and View Controller pairs. In Chapter 4, you learned how to port smaller individual components from the counterpart Android app, piece by piece. However, all those topics were designed to be self-contained without dependencies so they can serve as independent instructions.

In the real programming world, it is the combination of features and use cases that makes your app useful and entertaining. You will surely need more than one mapping guideline to complete a meaningful app. In this chapter, you are going to port an existing Android app from start to finish using the mapping topics from Chapters 3 and 4. Nothing will be new; you are still going to repeat the same top-down development approach as you have been using, and implement one piece at a time.

Perhaps there is one thing new that I have not yet mentioned explicitly: which piece should go first, and then what goes next. For any app, including the Android apps from which you are porting, you must go through the same thinking process. If you remember how you created the Android apps you are porting, that will be a great start because it will make your porting tasks to iOS more efficient. Otherwise, you will use the same thinking process that you normally use: decide the dependencies among the pieces and try to reduce the dependencies along the way. After all, there is really no absolutely right or wrong way. This is off our porting topic, but I think you will begin to understand my thinking process in this final exercise.

Again, to show and learn by example, your goal is to port an Android app, RentalROI, to iOS. Figure 5-1 shows the Android app you're porting.

Figure 5-1. Android RentalROI screens

This Android app performs the following tasks:

■ Every time a user enters new rental property parameters, user input is saved using SharedPreferences.

■ The amortization schedule is calculated on the remote server. The Android client simply calls the remote service to get the amortization schedules and stores the data locally.

■ If a saved amortization schedule exists, the app uses it instead of making a remote service call.

You will port this Android app to iOS and preserve the design decisions already made.

> **Note** This is just for exercise purposes. It would be better to calculate the amortization schedules locally without using the remote service—then you wouldn't need to persist the result.

You can download the ADT project from http://pdachoice.com/bookassets/RentalROI-adt.zip.

First, you'll create a new Xcode project using the Single View Application template, and give it the same name as the Android app: RentalROI. You will be following the same porting approaches you used in Chapters 3 ("Structure Your App") and 4 ("Implement Piece by Piece").

Structure Your App

Your first step is to create the Xcode storyboard as instructed in Chapter 3:

- Draw the storyboard scenes for each content view and connect UI widgets to the custom `UIViewController` that pairs with the storyboard scenes.

- Choose a navigation pattern and connect storyboard scenes together with segues.

This will result in a runnable iOS app with all the content views and the view controller classes' skeletons connected using the appropriate screen navigation pattern.

Draw Storyboard Scenes

You can clearly see four content views in Figure 5-1, and you will need to draw four storyboard scenes in `Main.storyboard`. You should use the counterpart ADT project as your live wireframe to create the iOS storyboard:

1. In no particular order, let's start with the simplest one, the `EditTextViewFragment` in the counterpart ADT project. The content view layout has only one `EditText` in the counterpart ADT project. You want to add a `UITextField` to the storyboard scene (see Chapter 4, "UITextField" for the detailed instructions).

    a. Drag a `UITextField` from **Object Library** to the View, and update its attributes in the **Attributes Inspector** as shown in Figure 5-2.

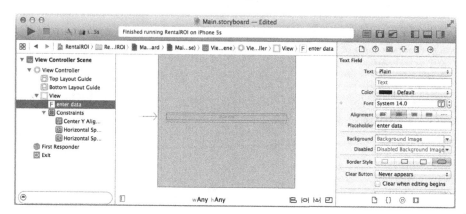

Figure 5-2. EditTextView storyboard scene

b. Center it vertically and add some space to the leading and trailing spaces (e.g., 20).

c. Create a bare-bones Swift `EditTextViewController` class that extends from `UIViewController` (see Listing 5-1).

d. To pair with the storyboard scene, enter the custom class name in the **Identity Inspector**.

e. In the **Connections Inspector**, connect the delegate outlet and New Referencing Outlet to your code.

Listing 5-1. EditTextViewController

```
import UIKit

class EditTextViewController: UIViewController, UITextFieldDelegate {
  @IBOutlet weak var mEditText: UITextField!
}
```

Continue drawing the next content view in no particular order, (e.g., the Property screen). In the Android counterpart `RentalPropertyViewFragment` class, I used `ListFragment` to achieve the L&F. In iOS, your natural choice is `UITableViewController` (see Chapter 3, "UITableViewController" for the detailed instructions).

a. Drag a `UITableViewController` from the **Object Library** and drop it onto the storyboard editor to create a storyboard scene.

b. Select the Table View and update the `Style` attribute to `Grouped` in **Attributes Inspector** (see Figure 5-3).

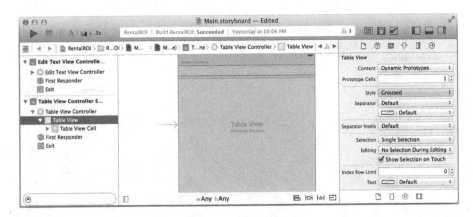

Figure 5-3. Creating a Table View scene

    c. Select the Table View Cell and update the attributes in **Attributes Inspector** (see Figure 5-4):

         ▨ Style: Select **Right Detail**.

         ▨ Identifier: Enter aCell.

Figure 5-4. Right Detail, Table View Cell

    d. Create a bare-bones Swift RentalPropertyViewController class that extends from UITableViewController (see Listing 5-2). To pair with the storyboard scene, enter the custom class name in the **Identity Inspector**.

Listing 5-2. RentalPropertyViewController

```
import UIKit
class RentalPropertyViewController: UITableViewController {

}
```

2. Continue drawing the next content view in no particular order (e.g., the Amortization screen). The counterpart Android AmortizationViewFragment is a standard ListFragment. Again, in iOS your natural choice for this is UITableViewController.

    a. Drag a UITableViewController from **Object Library** and drop it onto the storyboard editor to create a storyboard scene.

    b. Select the Table View Cell. In the **Attributes Inspector**, update the following attributes:

         ▨ Style: Select **Subtitle**.

         ▨ Identifier: Enter aCell.

    c. Create a bare-bones Swift AmortizationViewController class that extends from UITableViewController (see Listing 5-3).

    d.   To pair with the storyboard scene, enter the custom class name in the **Identity Inspector**.

Listing 5-3. AmortizationViewController

```
import UIKit
class AmortizationViewController: UITableViewController {


}
```

3.   Move on to the draw the last content view, Monthly Details. The counterpart Android `MonthlyTermViewFragment` layout looks like a `ListView` but actually was implemented with two `TextViews` and a decorated divider `View` for each line. You can translate these Android widgets piece by piece to iOS, or you can choose to use `UITableView` as in Step 2. In iOS, there is actually a better choice: using `UITableViewController` with static cells, each static cell for each line.

    a.   Drag a `UITableViewController` from `Object Library` and drop it onto the storyboard editor to create a storyboard scene.

    b.   Select the Table View to update the attributes in the **Attributes Inspector** as shown in Figure 5-5.

       ■ Content: Select **Static Cells**.

       ■ Sections: 2

       ■ Style: Select **Grouped**.

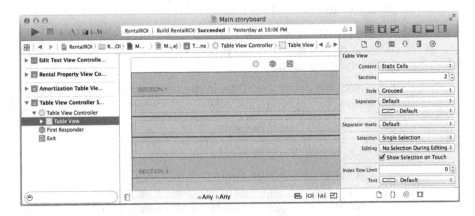

Figure 5-5. Static Cells Table View

4. The Monthly Details screen contains
   Mortgage Payment and Investment sections. You
   need to update the section title and add Table View
   Cells to both sections as shown in Figure 5-6.

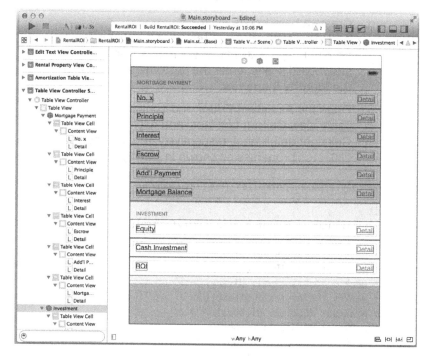

Figure 5-6. Two sections in the Monthly Details screen

a. To update the section title, select the **Table View
   Section** and update the Header attributes in
   Attributes Inspector:

   ■ Section 1: Mortgage Payment

   ■ Section 2: Investment

b. Since all of the Table View Cells in this view are
   designed to have the same style, it is easier just to
   create one and duplicate it. You may keep the first
   Table View Cell and delete the rest.

c. Select the Table View Cell and update the **Style** to
   Right Detail.

d. Select the Mortgage Payment section and update
   number of Rows to 6.

e. You need three Table View Cells for Section 2. You may repeat the preceding steps, or copy and paste in the storyboard editor.

f. Update all the Table View Cell titles as shown in the counterpart Android content view.

g. Create a bare-bones Swift MonthlyTermViewController class that extends from UITableViewController. To pair with the storyboard scene, enter the custom class name in the **Identity Inspector**.

h. Open the **Assistant Editor** and connect the first Table View Cell left text label and each Table View Cell right detail label, respectively, to your code's IBOutlet properties as shown in Listing 5-4.

Listing 5-4. MonthlyTermViewController IBOutlet Properties

```
import UIKit
class MonthlyTermViewController : UITableViewController {

    @IBOutlet weak var mPaymentNo: UILabel!
    @IBOutlet weak var mTotalPmt: UILabel!
    @IBOutlet weak var mPrincipal: UILabel!
    @IBOutlet weak var mInterest: UILabel!
    @IBOutlet weak var mEscrow: UILabel!
    @IBOutlet weak var mAddlPmt: UILabel!
    @IBOutlet weak var mBalance: UILabel!
    @IBOutlet weak var mEquity: UILabel!
    @IBOutlet weak var mCashInvested: UILabel!
    @IBOutlet weak var mRoi: UILabel!
}
```

Figure 5-7 depicts the storyboard scenes translated from the Android counterparts.

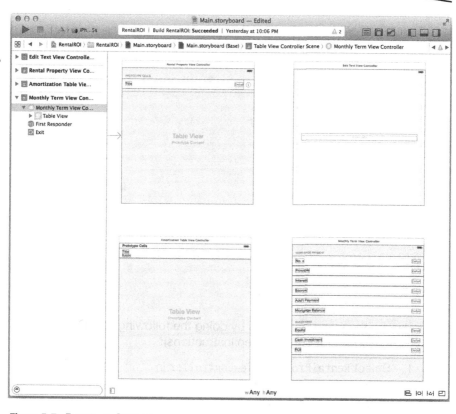

Figure 5-7. *Four RentalROI scenes*

Choose a Screen Navigation Pattern

When choosing appropriate navigation pattern(s), you will naturally get a very good idea by playing with the Android app from which you're porting. Sometimes you may need more than one pattern, such as a Navigation Stack plus Navigation Tabs. In this RentalROI app, you want to be able go back to a previous scene from the Monthly Details to Amortization List to Property Detail screens. The popular Navigation Stack navigation pattern is prefect for this intended behavior (see Chapter 3, "Navigation Stack"). For going to and from the Edit Text scene, you can choose a different navigation pattern that shows a stronger relationship to the originating context. Dialog or the iOS Popover is the choice (see Chapter 3, "UIPopoverController").

Your immediate mission is to add the navigation patterns and draw storyboard segues to connect all the storyboard scenes to one another. Figure 5-8 shows the final storyboard with all the scenes connected.

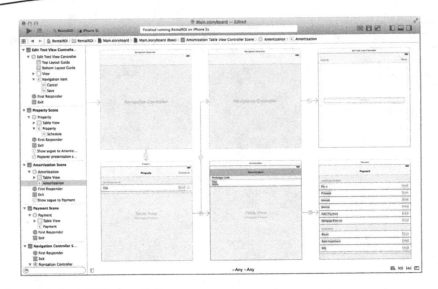

Figure 5-8. RentalROI connected scenes

Continue with the storyboard tasks by doing the following (see Chapter 3, "Storyboard Segue" for step-by-step instructions):

1. Select `RentalPropertyViewController` in the storyboard editor and embed it in a `UINavigationController` (see Figure 3-33 in Chapter 3, "UINavigationController" for detailed instructions).

   a. Make sure Is Initial View Controller is checked in the Navigation Controller **Attributes Inspector**.

   b. Select the Navigation Item in the `RentalPropertyViewController` to update the Title attribute to `Property` in **Attributes Inspector**.

   c. Add a right `BarButtonItem` to the `Property` Navigation Item in `RentalPropertyViewController`. Also update the button Title attribute to Schedule in the `BarButtonItem` **Attributes Inspector**.

   d. Connect the Schedule `BarButtonItem` action outlet in **Connections Inspector** to your code, such as `doSchedule(...)`.

2. Connect a Manual Segue from `RentalPropertyViewController` to `AmortizationViewController`.

    a. Segue: Show (e.g., Push).

    b. Identifier: AmortizationTable.

3. Connect a Manual Segue from RentalPropertyViewController to EditTextViewController.

    a. Segue: Present As Popover.

    b. Identifier: EditText.

    c. Anchor: Table View.

    d. Directions: none (uncheck all).

4. Connect a Manual Segue from AmortizationViewController to MonthlyTermViewController.

    a. Segue: Show (e.g., Push).

    b. Identifier: MonthlyTerm.

5. Add Navigation Item to AmortizationViewController and MonthlyTermViewController as shown in Figure 5-8.

    a. Drag Navigation Item from **Object Libraries** and drop it onto the controller in the storyboard document outline.

    b. Update the Navigation Item Title respectively (e.g., Amortization and Payment).

6. Since you are not showing the EditTextViewController with the navigation pattern, EditTextViewController doesn't have a Navigation Item for Title or BarButtonItem like the rest of the storyboard scenes. You may either draw a UINavigationBar from **Object Libraries**, or more commonly, you can simply embed it in another UINavigationController.

    a. Select the view controller and select **Editor ➤ Embedded In ➤ Navigation Controller** from the Xcode **Editor** menu.

    b. Add a right BarButtonItem. Update the Title attribute to be Save and connect the action outlet to your code, such as doSave(...).

    c.   Add a left BarButtonItem. Update the Title
       attribute to be Cancel and connect the action outlet
       to your code, such as doCancel(...).

You should have a storyboard with all scenes connected with segues as
shown in Figure 5-8.

Implement Piece by Piece

Let's take a look at the pieces you have now. Figure 5-9 shows the
structures of both projects side by side.

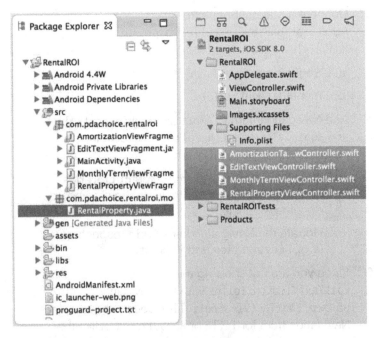

Figure 5-9. Android and iOS RentalROI project structures

The iOS ViewController classes are in place and mapped one-to-one
with the Android counterpart Fragments. There is one model class,
RentalProperty, not in the iOS project yet. Let's create a Swift class
skeleton for the RentalProperty model class (see Listing 5-5) first.

Listing 5-5. RentalProperty.swift Skeleton

```
import Foundation
public class RentalProperty {

}
```

Application Resources

Same as Android apps, most iOS apps need images or digital assets to dress up the whole app. Also, you definitely want to port the externalized text to iOS. Do the following to port the application resources (see Chapter 4, "Application Resources") from the Android counterpart to iOS:

1. Translate the Android `strings.xml` to iOS:

    a. In Xcode, select the `Supporting Files` folder to create a new file (⌘+N) in it, and follow the on-screen instructions to select **iOS ➤ Resource ➤ Strings File**. Name it: `Localizable.strings`.

    b. Copy the content in Android `res/values/strings.xml` to the iOS `Localizable.strings` file. The translation is straightforward, as shown in Listing 5-6.

Listing 5-6. Externalized Text Translation

```
"app_name" = "RentalROI";
"label_schedule" = "Schedule";
"label_property" = "Property";
"label_Amortization" = "Amortization";
"label_monthlydetails" = "Monthly Details";
"button_next" = "Next";

/* RentalPropertyView */
"mortgage" = "MORTGAGE";
"operations" = "OPERATIONS";
"purchasePrice" = "Purchase Price";
"downPayment" = "Down Payment %";
"loanAmount" = "Loan Amount";
"interestRate" = "Interest Rate %";
"mortgageTerm" = "Mortgage Term (Yr.)";
"escrowAmount" = "Escrow Amount";
"extraPayment" = "Extra Payment";
"expenses" = "Expenses";
"rent" = "Rent";

/* EditTextView */
"save" = "Save";
"editTextSize" = "15";

/* Monthly Details */
"MortgagePayment" = "MORTGAGE PAYMENT";
"no" = "No.";
"Principal" = "Principal";
"interest" = "Interest";
```

```
"escrow" = "Escrow";
"addlPayment" = "Add\'l Payment";
"mortgageBalance" = "Mortgage Balance";
"equity" = "Equity";
"cashInvest" = "Cash Investment";
"roi" = "ROI";
```

2. Generally, you reuse or recreate digital assets from your Android project. In this app, you only have one: the application icon, ic_launcher.png.

   a. Create ic_launcher120.png, ic_launcher180.png, ic_launcher76.png, and ic_launcher152.png from the Android project res/xxhdpi/ic_launcher.png file.

   b. Select Images.xcassets and AppIcon in the Xcode asset catalog and drag the four files you just made as shown in Figure 5-10: ic_launcher120.png for iPhone 2x, ic_launcher180.png for iPhone 3x, ic_launcher76.png for iPad 1x and ic_launcher152.png for iPad 2x. The image resolution must match exactly or Xcode will give you warnings.

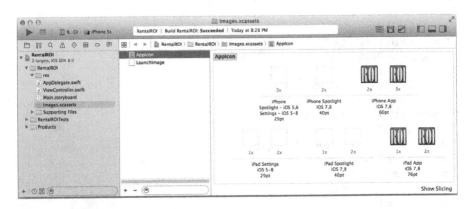

Figure 5-10. *Xcode project* AppIcon

If the Android app contains resources for I18N, you want to port them to the iOS app as well.

Java Class to Swift Class

Now, you have all the matching classes in your Xcode iOS project. Your next step is to break each class into more pieces, porting Android methods to iOS methods. Again, I use a top-down approach in each class: port the member signatures first, and try to defer the internal implementations as late as possible. For your convenience, you may use Table 5-1 as a step-by-step guide. You will find that the information in the table is common sense after one or more exercises, but I think it makes translation efforts more systematic.

Table 5-1. Class Porting Steps

Step	Instructions
1.	For each class, copy the contents of the Java counterpart to Swift.
2.	Translate Java fields to Swift Stored Properties. For Java static constants, translate them to Swift inner `struct` `static` variables.
3.	Translate the method declarations to Swift. Preserve signatures as much as possible except those that are life cycle methods.
	a. Keep the Java impl as Swift comments. They are perfect and tested logics.
	b. Translate Android life cycle methods signature to iOS counterparts including constructors.
	c. Preserve utility methods signatures.

Steps 1 and 2 are straightforward. Step 3 is the key to break the class into smaller pieces: methods. After you run down all the classes with Table 5-1, all the classes should have callable method skeletons. You can start to translate the commented Java code to Swift in each method one by one (see "Java Methods to Swift Methods" later in this chapter).

For your convenience, Table 5-2 recaps the member declarations mappings that you will surely encounter in this step.

Table 5-2. Member declarations in Java and Swift

Languages	Java	Swift
Variables	`String aName`	`var aName: String`
Class variable	`static ...`	static var in inner struct
Method declaration	`String aMethod(int a)`	`func aMethod(a: Int) -> String`
Class method	`static ...`	`class func ...`
Constructor	`ClassName(...)`	`init(...)`
Android Context	`Activity, Context`	Remove them.

Model Class: RentalProperty

A great deal of the translation effort involves converting the general Java-to-Swift language programming rules (see Table 2-1). Your immediate goal is to port the counterpart Java class `RentalProperty` members to Swift without renaming them. For methods, focus on signatures by commenting all the implementation code. Follow the class porting steps in Table 5-1 to port `RentalProperty.java` to Swift:

1. To start, copy the whole `RentalProperty.java` class to the `RentalProperty.swift` file. You will get a *lot* of errors. These compilations errors are your free guidance.

2. Next, define the classes. A general rule of thumb: keep any signature including class name. The caller and callee will just connect without glitches in later steps. Delete or comment out pure Java things, i.e., `implements Serializable` (see Listing 5-7).

Listing 5-7. RentalProperty.swift Class Declaration

```
public class RentalProperty /* implements Serializable */ {
// private static final long serialVersionUID = 1L;
  ...
}
```

3. Translate Java fields to Swift:

> **Tip**   Java: `String mProperty;` => Swift: `var mProperty: String`
>
> Or, `var mProperty = ""`   `// use type inference when possible`

   a.   Java fields to Swift Stored Properties (see Listing 5-8).

   b.   Java `static` variables to Swift inner `struct` `static` variables.

Listing 5-8. RentalProperty.swift Stored Properties

```
public class RentalProperty /* implements Serializable */ {
  ...
// private double purchasePrice;
// private double loanAmt;
// private double interestRate;
// private int numOfTerms;
// private double escrow;
// private double extra;
// private double expenses;
// private double rent;
  var purchasePrice = 0.0;
  var loanAmt = 0.0;
  var interestRate = 5.0;
  var numOfTerms = 30;
  var escrow = 0.0;
  var extra = 0.0;
  var expenses = 0.0;
  var rent = 0.0;

// public static final String KEY_AMO_SAVED = "KEY_AMO_SAVED";
// public static final String KEY_PROPERTY = "KEY_PROPERTY";
// private static final String PREFS_NAME = "MyPrefs";
// private static final int MODE = Context.MODE_PRIVATE;
    // MODE_WORLD_WRITEABLE
// private static RentalProperty _sharedInstance = null;
  struct MyStatic {
    static let KEY_AMO_SAVED = "KEY_AMO_SAVED";
    static let KEY_PROPERTY = "KEY_PROPERTY";
    private static let PREFS_NAME = "MyPrefs";
    private static let MODE = 0; // probably Android thing
    private static var _sharedInstance = RentalProperty()
  }
  ...
}
```

4. Translate the method declarations to Swift, as shown
    in Listing 5-9. Preserve signatures as much as
    possible except those that are life cycle methods.

> **Tip**   Java: `String doWork(int param);` => Swift: `func doWork(Int: Type) -> String`

   a. Keep the Java impl as Swift comments. They are
    perfect/tested logics.

   b. Translate Android life cycle methods signatures to
    iOS counterparts including constructors.

   c. Preserve utility methods signatures.

   d. You can safely delete the Android `Context` (or any
    pure Android or Java specifics).

> **Note**   Conventionally, you don't need to port the Java field accessors. I choose to port them now just because they are used by Java callers a lot. I normally remove/refactor these Java-ish accessors after the app is working.

Listing 5-9. Porting RentalProperty Methods

```swift
class RentalProperty {
    ...
// private RentalProperty() {
  private init() {
    // Commented Java code omitted
  }

// public static RentalProperty sharedInstance() {
  class func sharedInstance() -> RentalProperty {
    // Commented Java code omitted
    return RentalProperty()
  }

// public String getAmortizationPersistentKey() {
  func getAmortizationPersistentKey() -> String {
```

```
  // Commented Java code omitted
     return ""
  }

// public JSONArray getSavedAmortization(Context activity) {
   func getSavedAmortization() -> NSArray? {
     // Commented Java code omitted
     return nil
  }

// public boolean saveAmortization(String data, Context activity){
   func saveAmortization(data: NSArray) -> Bool {
     // Commented Java code omitted
     return false
  }

// public boolean load(Context activity) {
   func load() -> Bool {
     // Commented Java code omitted
     return true
  }

// public boolean save(Context activity) {
   func save() -> Bool {
     // Commented Java code omitted
     return true
  }

//////////// SharedPreferences usage /////////////////////
// public boolean saveSharedPref(String key, String data, Context activity) {
   func saveSharedPref(key:String,data:AnyObject)->Bool{
     // Commented Java code omitted
     return true
  }

// public String retrieveSharedPref(String key, Context activity) {
   func retrieveSharedPref(key: String) -> AnyObject? {
     // Commented Java code omitted
     return nil
  }

// public void deleteSharedPref(String key, Context activity) {
   func deleteSharedPref(key: String) {
     // Commented Java code omitted
  }
```

```
// JavaBean accessors
func getPurchasePrice()-> Double {
  return self.purchasePrice;
}

func setPurchasePrice(purchasePrice: Double) {
  self.purchasePrice = purchasePrice;
}

func getLoanAmt()-> Double {
  return self.loanAmt;
}

func setLoanAmt(loanAmt: Double) {
  self.loanAmt = loanAmt;
}

func getInterestRate()-> Double {
  return self.interestRate;
}

func setInterestRate(interestRate: Double) {
  self.interestRate = interestRate;
}

func getNumOfTerms()-> Int {
  return self.numOfTerms;
}

func setNumOfTerms(numOfTerms: Int) {
  self.numOfTerms = numOfTerms;
}

func getEscrow()-> Double {
  return self.escrow;
}

func setEscrow(escrow: Double) {
  self.escrow = escrow;
}

func getExtra()-> Double {
  return self.extra;
}

func setExtra(extra: Double) {
  self.extra = extra;
}
```

```
func getExpenses()-> Double {
  return self.expenses;
}

func setExpenses(expenses: Double) {
  self.expenses = expenses;
}

func getRent()-> Double {
  return self.rent;
}

func setRent(rent: Double) {
  self.rent = rent;
}
...
```

You have achieved the immediate goal.

> **Note**   You really cannot get any better method comments than these, because they are actually code that has been proven to work.

EditTextViewController

ANDROID ANALOGY

The iOS counterpart is `EditTextViewFragment`.

Let's start on the first view controller, `EditTextViewController`.

> **Note**   I would've chosen `RentalPropertyController` first if it didn't need `EditTextViewController`. The dependencies can be easily seen in the counterpart Java packages' import statements. You may choose any one to start with and bear with those temporary compilation errors.

Your immediate goal is to translate the Android `EditTextViewFragment` Java class definitions and member signatures to iOS Swift classes. Again, copy the whole `EditTextViewFragment.java` class onto the existing `EditTextViewController.swift` class to start with:

1. Start with the class-level definition. There is an inner interface, but Swift doesn't have inner protocol. You can safely create the protocol in the same file outside of the class definition as shown in Listing 5-10.

Listing 5-10. Java Interface to Swift Protocol

```
// Java interface to Swift protocol
protocol EditTextViewControllerDelegate {
  func onTextEditSaved(tag: Int, text: String);
  func onTextEditCanceled();
}

class EditTextViewController : UIViewController, UITextFieldDelegate {
  ...
//// inner interface
//  interface EditTextViewControllerDelegate {
//    public void onTextEditSaved(int tag, String text);
//    public void onTextEditCanceled();
//  }
  ...
```

2. Translate Java fields to Swift (see Listing 5-11):

    a. Java fields to Swift Stored Properties.

    b. Most likely, the Java fields related to UI widgets are the existing IBOutlet properties.

Listing 5-11. Java Fields to Swift Stored Properties

```
class EditTextViewController : ... {
  ...
// private int editTextTag;
// private String header;
// private String text;
// private EditTextViewControllerDelegate delegate;
// private View contentView; => in super.view already
// private EditText mEditText; => existing IBOutlet
  var editTextTag = 0
  var header = ""
  var text = ""
  var delegate: EditTextViewControllerDelegate!
  ...
```

3. Translate the method declarations to Swift (see
    Listing 5-12). Preserve signatures except those that
    are life cycle methods.

    a. Keep the Java impl as Swift comments. They are
        perfect/tested logics.

    b. Translate Android Fragment life cycle method
        signatures to iOS counterpart View life cycle
        methods.

    c. Preserve utility method signatures.

    d. You can safely delete the Android Context (or any
        pure Android or Java specifics).

    e. You don't need those conventional Java bean
        accessors in Swift.

Listing 5-12. EditTextViewController Life Cycle Callbacks

```
class EditTextViewController : ... {
  ...
// @Override public View onCreateView(...) {
  override func viewDidLoad() {
    // Commented Java code omitted
  }

// @Override public void onResume() {
  override func viewDidAppear(animated: Bool) {
    // Commented Java code omitted
  }

// @Override public void onPause() {
  override func viewWillDisappear(animated: Bool) {
    // Commented Java code omitted
  }

// @Override public void onCreateOptionsMenu(...) {
  // the navigationBar already drawn in storyboard

// @Override public boolean onOptionsItemSelected(...) {
  // the IBActions: doSave and doCancel

// private void showKeyboard() {
  func showKeyboard(){
    // Commented Java code omitted
  }
```

```
// private void hideKeyboard() {
  func hideKeyboard() {
    // Commented Java code omitted
  }
  // public accessors, not needed in Swift
  ...
```

RentalPropertyViewController

IOS ANALOGY

The ADT counterpart is `RentalPropertyViewFragment`.

Move on to the next view controller: `RentalPropertyViewController`. Copy the `RentalPropertyViewFragment` Java class onto the existing `RentalPropertyViewController.swift` class. Use the porting steps in Table 5-1 and do the following:

1. Start with the class-level definition. `ListFragment` naturally maps to iOS `UITableViewController` (see Listing 5-13).

Listing 5-13. Java Interface to Swift Protocol

```
// public class RentalPropertyViewFragment extends ListFragment
// implements EditTextViewControllerDelegate
class RentalPropertyViewController: UITableViewController,
EditTextViewControllerDelegate {
  ...
```

2. Translate Java fields to Swift (see Listing 5-14):

    a. Java fields to Swift Stored Properties.

    b. Most likely, the UI widgets' related Java fields are already the existing `IBOutlet` properties.

    c. Swift doesn't support class-type variables yet. Create an inner `struct` for those Java `final` constants.

Listing 5-14. Java Fields to Swift Stored Properties

```
class RentalPropertyViewController: ... {
  ...
///// from Java counterpart
//private static let URL_service_tmpl = "http://www.pdachoice.com/ras/
service/amortization?loan=%.2f&rate=%.3f&terms=%d&extra=%.2f&escrow=%.2f"
// private static final String KEY_DATA = "data";
// private static final String KEY_RC = "rc";
// private static final String KEY_ERROR = "error";
  struct MyStatic {
    private static let URL_service_tmpl = "http://www.pdachoice.
    com/ras/service/amortization?loan=%.2f&rate=%.3f&terms=%d&ext
    ra=%.2f&escrow=%.2f"
    private static let KEY_DATA = "data"
    private static let KEY_RC = "rc"
    private static let KEY_ERROR = "error"
  }

// private RentalProperty _property;
// private JSONArray _savedAmortization;
// private BaseAdapter mAdapter; // pure Android
  var _property = RentalProperty.sharedInstance()
  var _savedAmortization: NSArray?
  ...
```

3. Translate the method declarations to Swift as shown in Listing 5-15:

   a. Keep the Java impl as Swift comments. They are perfect/tested logics.

   b. Translate Android Fragment life cycle method signatures to iOS counterpart View life cycle methods.

   c. Preserve utility methods signatures.

   d. Translate Android BaseAdapter to iOS DataSource impl.

Listing 5-15. EditTextViewController Life Cycle Callbacks

```
class RentalPropertyViewController: ... {
  ...
///// from Java counterpart
// @Override public void onCreate(Bundle savedInstanceState) {
  override func viewDidLoad() {
    // Commented Java code omitted
  }
```

```
// @Override public void onResume() {
  override func viewDidAppear(animated: Bool) {
    // Commented Java code omitted
  }

//  @Override public void onCreateOptionsMenu(...) {
  // UINavigationBar already drawn in storyboard

//  @Override public boolean onOptionsItemSelected(...) {
  @IBAction func doSchedule(sender: AnyObject) {
    // Commented Java code omitted
    self.performSegueWithIdentifier("AmortizationTable", sender: sender)
  }

//// callback method when list item is selected.
// @Override public void onListItemClick(...) {
  override func tableView(tableView: UITableView, didSelectRowAtIndexPath
indexPath: NSIndexPath) {
    // Commented Java code omitted
  }
//private BaseAdapter createListAdapter() {
// Commented Java code omitted  }
  override func tableView(tableView: UITableView, numberOfRowsInSection
section: Int) -> Int {
    // TODO: Android Adapter to iOS DataSource impl later
    return 0
  }

  override func numberOfSectionsInTableView(tableView: UITableView) -> Int {
    // TODO: Android Adapter to iOS DataSource impl later
    return 0
  }

  override func tableView(tableView: UITableView, cellForRowAtIndexPath
indexPath: NSIndexPath) -> UITableViewCell {
    // TODO: Android Adapter to iOS DataSource impl later
    return UITableViewCell()
  }

//// delegate interface
// public void onTextEditSaved(int tag, String text) {
  func onTextEditSaved(tag: Int, text: String) {
    // Commented Java code omitted
  }

// public void onTextEditCanceled() {
  func onTextEditCanceled() {
    // Commented Java code omitted
  }
```

```
// public void doAmortization(Object sender) {
  func doAmortization() {
    // Commented Java code omitted
  }

//// GET data from url
// private JSONObject httpGet(String myurl) {
  private func httpGet(myurl: String) -> NSDictionary? {
      // Commented Java code omitted
return [:]
  }

// private String readStream(InputStream stream) {
  func readStream(stream: NSInputStream) -> String {
    // Commented Java code omitted
    return ""
  }
  ...
```

> **Note**   It is all about the same idea: move the code from the Android
> counterpart; translation will be done in a top-down fashion. In other words,
> get the Swift classes in place first, and then get the Swift method stubs in
> place with precise comments written in the tested Android code.

AmortizationViewController

```
                          IOS ANALOGY
```

The ADT counterpart is AmortizationViewFragment.

Move on to the next view controller: AmortizationViewController. Follow
the porting steps in Table 5-1; Listing 5-16 shows the intermediate results.

Listing 5-16. AmortizationViewController Properties and Method Signatures

```
class AmortizationViewController : UITableViewController {

///// from Java counterpart
// private JSONArray monthlyTerms;
// private BaseAdapter mAdapter;
  var monthlyTerms = NSArray()
```

```
// @Override public void onCreate(Bundle savedInstanceState) {
  override func viewDidLoad() {
    // Commented Java code omitted
  }

  override func tableView(tableView: UITableView, numberOfRowsInSection
section: Int) -> Int {
    // TODO: Android Adapter to iOS DataSource impl later
    return 0
  }

  override func tableView(tableView: UITableView, cellForRowAtIndexPath
indexPath: NSIndexPath) -> UITableViewCell {
    // TODO Android Adapter to iOS DataSource impl later
    return UITableViewCell()
  }

// @Override public void onResume() {
  override func viewDidAppear(animated: Bool) {
    // Commented Java code omitted
  }

// public void onListItemClick(...) {
  override func tableView(tableView: UITableView, didSelectRowAtIndexPath
indexPath: NSIndexPath) {
    // Commented Java code omitted
  }
}
```

MonthlyTermViewFragment

IOS ANALOGY

The ADT counterpart is `MonthlyTermViewFragment`.

The `MonthlyTermViewController` is the last view controller. Follow the porting steps in Table 5-1; Listing 5-17 shows the intermediate results.

Listing 5-17. MonthlyTermViewController Properties and Method Signatures

```
class MonthlyTermViewController : UITableViewController {

  @IBOutlet weak var mPaymentNo: UILabel!
  @IBOutlet weak var mTotalPmt: UILabel!
  @IBOutlet weak var mPrincipal: UILabel!
  @IBOutlet weak var mInterest: UILabel!
  @IBOutlet weak var mEscrow: UILabel!
```

```
@IBOutlet weak var mAddlPmt: UILabel!
@IBOutlet weak var mBalance: UILabel!
@IBOutlet weak var mEquity: UILabel!
@IBOutlet weak var mCashInvested: UILabel!
@IBOutlet weak var mRoi: UILabel!

///// from Java counterpart
// private JSONObject monthlyTerm;
  var monthlyTerm = NSDictionary()

//// IBOutlets above, and super.view
// private TextView mPaymentNo;
// private TextView mTotalPmt;
// private TextView mPrincipal;
// private TextView mInterest;
// private TextView mEscrow;
// private TextView mAddlPmt;
// private TextView mBalance;
// private TextView mEquity;
// private TextView mCashInvested;
// private TextView mRoi;
// private View contentView;

// @Override public View onCreateView(...) {
  override func viewDidLoad() {
    // Commented Java code omitted
  }

// @Override public void onResume() {
  override func viewDidAppear(animated: Bool) {
    // Commented Java code omitted
  }

// JavaBean accessors => not needed with Swift properties
}
```

Unlike UITableViewController with dynamic cells, you don't need to provide the Data Source. This is the last class. You should have all the classes that contain properties and methods that can be called from other classes. In other words, the programming interface is in place.

Java Methods to Swift Methods

You already broke each class into more pieces—that is, methods. The last step to complete your iOS project is to fully implement each method by translating from the commented Java code. The language syntax invoking methods in Swift is the same as Java. Except for the code using the Android-specific API, most of the Java code should work in Swift! For the code using Android-specific APIs, use Chapter 4 to guide you through your translating efforts.

Programming languages naturally embed rules. For your convenience, Table 5-3 lists some common types or syntax in both languages.

Table 5-3. Replaceable Java to Swift Syntax or Symbols

Item	Java	Swift
Self	`this.aMember`	`self.aMember`
Variables	`String aName`	`var aName: String`
Boolean	`boolean`	`Bool`
Integer	`Integer or int`	`Int, UInt`
Null value	`null`	`nil`
Array	`ArrayList or JSONArray if string` serialization is required	`Array or NSArray`
Hash table	`HashMap or JSONObject if string` serialization is required	`Dictionary or NSDictionary`

Note that you can always use **Find** and **Replace** (⌘F) in the Xcode editor, or the **Find Navigator** to replace repeatable patterns in the whole project. Figure 5-11 depicts an example.

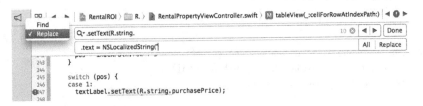

Figure 5-11. Find and Replace in Xcode editor

EditTextViewController

Now move on to the first view controller, `EditTextViewController`. In the ADT project, this counterpart Android `Fragment` only has a `EditText` that presents the text for editing from the presenting `Fragment`. It also displays the name of the text on the title. When the user saves or cancels the edit operations, the modified text is returned to the presenting `Fragment`. Do the following to port the same functionalities to iOS:

1. Translate the Android life cycle methods to iOS counterparts, `IBAction` methods, and other matching methods (see Listing 5-18). The Android action items in **Options Menu** are translated to iOS barButtonItems on the Navigation Bar. Connect the **Save** and **Cancel** buttons to your IBAction methods; for example, `doSave()` and `doCancel()`.

Listing 5-18. EditTextViewController Life Cycle Callbacks

```
class EditTextViewController : UIViewController, UITextFieldDelegate {
  ...
  override func viewDidLoad() {
//  contentView = inflater.inflate(...);
//  setHasOptionsMenu(true); // enable Option Menu.
//  mEditText = (EditText) contentView.findViewById(...);
//  this.mEditText.setText(this.text);
//  getActivity().setTitle(header);
//  return contentView;
    super.viewDidLoad()
    mEditText.text = self.text
    self.navigationItem.title = self.header
  }

  override func viewDidAppear(animated: Bool) {
//  super.onResume();
//  ((MainActivity) getActivity()).slideIn(...);
//  showKeyboard();
    super.viewDidAppear(animated)
    showKeyboard()
  }

  override func viewWillDisappear(animated: Bool) {
//  super.onPause();
//  hideKeyboard();
    super.viewWillDisappear(animated)
    hideKeyboard()
  }

  override func viewDidDisappear(animated: Bool) {
//  super.onPause();
//  hideKeyboard();
    super.viewDidDisappear(animated)
  }

//  @Override
//  public boolean onOptionsItemSelected(...) {
//  String returnText = this.mEditText.getText().toString();
//  if(delegate != null) {
//  this.delegate.onTextEditSaved(this.getEditTextTag(),returnText);
//  }
//  return true;
//  }
```

```
@IBAction func doSave(sender: AnyObject) {
  var returnText = self.mEditText.text
  if(delegate != nil) {
    delegate.onTextEditSaved(self.editTextTag, text: returnText)
  }
}

@IBAction func doCancel(sender: AnyObject) {
  if(delegate != nil) {
    delegate.onTextEditCanceled()
  }
}

private func showKeyboard() {
// InputMethodManager imm = (InputMethodManager) ... ;
// imm.showSoftInput(...);
// mEditText.selectAll();
  self.mEditText.becomeFirstResponder()
}

private func hideKeyboard() {
// InputMethodManager imm = (InputMethodManager) ... ;
// imm.hideSoftInputFromWindow(...);
  self.mEditText.endEditing(true)
}
...
```

2. The soft keyboard does not behave the same.
    Keyboard implementation is very platform
    dependent. Unlike Android, which shifts the view up
    automatically when the keyboard appears, you need
    to write code to mimic the same behavior, as shown
    in Listing 5-19.

Listing 5-19. Keyboard Implementation

```
class EditTextViewController : ... {
  ...
  override func viewDidLoad() {
    ...
    if UIDevice.currentDevice().userInterfaceIdiom == .Phone {
      NSNotificationCenter.defaultCenter().addObserver(self,
          selector: "keyboardAppeared:", name:
UIKeyboardDidShowNotification, object: nil)
    }
  }
```

```
override func viewDidDisappear(animated: Bool) {
  ...
  NSNotificationCenter.defaultCenter().removeObserver(self)
}

func keyboardAppeared(notification: NSNotification) {
  var keyboardInfo = notification.userInfo as NSDictionary!
  var kbFrame = keyboardInfo.valueForKey(UIKeyboardFrameBeginUs erInfoKey)
  as NSValue
  var kbFrameRect: CGRect = kbFrame.CGRectValue()
  var keyboardH = min(kbFrameRect.size.width, kbFrameRect.size.height)
  var screenRect: CGRect = UIScreen.mainScreen().bounds;

  var tfRect: CGRect = self.mEditText.frame
  var y = screenRect.size.height - keyboardH - mEditText.frame.
  size.height - 20
  var x = (screenRect.size.width - tfRect.size.width) / 2

  UIView.animateWithDuration(0.1, animations: { () -> Void in
    var newRect = CGRectMake(x, y, tfRect.size.width, tfRect.size.height);
    self.mEditText.frame = newRect
  })
}
...
```

RentalPropertyViewController

When the app is launched, this is the first content view. The purpose of this view controller is to collect user input. Do the following to port the implementation from Android to iOS:

1. Translate the life cycle methods, as shown in Listing 5-20.

   a. Same as in Android, always call super.viewXXX.

   b. Remove the Android Options Menu code. You have an iOS-drawn NavigationController/NavigationBar in storyboard already (see Chapter 3).

Listing 5-20. Life Cycle Methods Implementation

```
class RentalPropertyViewController : UITableViewController {
  ...
  override func viewDidLoad() {
    super.viewDidLoad() // super.onCreate(savedInstanceState);
    _property = RentalProperty.sharedInstance();
    _property.load(/*getActivity()*/);
```

```
//    setHasOptionsMenu(true); // enable Option Menu.
//    mAdapter = createListAdapter();
//    this.setListAdapter(mAdapter);
  }

  override func viewDidAppear(animated: Bool) {
    super.viewDidAppear(animated) // super.onResume();
// getActivity().setTitle(getText(R.string.label_property));
    self.navigationItem.title = "Property"
  }

  @IBAction func doSchedule(sender: AnyObject) {
//    doAmortization();
    doAmortization()
  }
  ...
}
```

2. Translate the Android Adapter for ListFragment to
   iOS UITableViewDataSource as shown in Listing 5-21.
   Just for demonstrating how to reuse the Android
   BaseAdapter code more effectively, I chose to flatten
   the iOS cell section-row indexPath to the Android list
   view item position. For example, the UITableViewCell
   at the first row of the second section is the original
   Android list item at position 9.

Listing 5-21. Implement TableView DataSource

```
class RentalPropertyViewController : UITableViewController {
...
// private BaseAdapter createListAdapter() {
//   return new BaseAdapter() {
//
//     @Override
//     public int getItemViewType(int pos) {
//       if (pos == 0 || pos == 8) {
//         return 0;
//       } else {
//         return 1;
//       }
//     }
//
//     @Override
//     public int getViewTypeCount() {
//       return 2;
//     }
//
```

```
//     @Override
//     public View getView(int pos, ... ) {
//
//       if (view == null) {
//         LayoutInflater inflater = getActivity().getLayoutInflater();
//         if (pos == 0 || pos == 8) {
//           // header list item
//           view = inflater.inflate(android.R.layout.simple_list_item_1, null);
//         } else {
//           // right detail list item
//           view = inflater.inflate(R.layout.rightdetail_listitem, null);
//         }
//       }
//
//       if (pos == 0 || pos == 8) {
//         // header list item
//         view.setBackgroundColor(Color.argb(32, 0, 128, 128));
//         TextView text1 = (TextView) view.
//         findViewById(android.R.id.text1);
//
//         if (pos == 0) {
//           text1.setText(getResources().getString(R.string.mortgage));
//         } else {
//           text1.setText(getResources().getString(R.string.operations));
//         }
//       } else {
//         // right detail list item
//         view.setBackgroundColor(Color.argb(0, 0, 0, 0));
//         TextView textLabel = (TextView) view.findViewById (R.id.textLabel);
//         TextView detailTextLabel = (TextView) view.
//         findViewById(R.id.detailTextLabel);
//
//         switch (pos) {
//         case 1:
//           textLabel.setText(R.string.purchasePrice);
//           detailTextLabel.setText(String.format("%.0f",
//           _property.getPurchasePrice()));
//           break;
//         case 2:
//           textLabel.setText(R.string.downPayment);
//           if (_property.getPurchasePrice() > 0) {
//           double down = (1 - _property.getLoanAmt() /
//           _property.getPurchasePrice()) * 100.0f;
//             detailTextLabel.setText(String.format("%.0f",
//             down));//
//             if (_property.getLoanAmt() == 0 && down > 0) {
```

```
//                 _property.setLoanAmt(_property.getPurchasePrice()
//                  * (1 - down / 100.0f));
//               }
//           } else {
//             detailTextLabel.setText("0");
//           }
//           break;
//       case 3:
//           textLabel.setText(R.string.loanAmount);
//           detailTextLabel.setText(String.format("%.2f",
//           _property.getLoanAmt()));
//           break;
//       case 4:
//           textLabel.setText(R.string.interestRate);
//           detailTextLabel.setText(String.format("%.3f",
//           _property.getInterestRate()));
//           break;
//       case 5:
//           textLabel.setText(R.string.mortgageTerm);
//           detailTextLabel.setText(String.format("%d",
//           _property.getNumOfTerms()));
//           break;
//       case 6:
//           textLabel.setText(R.string.escrowAmount);
//           detailTextLabel.setText(String.format("%.0f",
//           _property.getEscrow()));
//           break;
//       case 7:
//           textLabel.setText(R.string.extraPayment);
//           detailTextLabel.setText(String.format("%.0f",
//           _property.getExtra()));
//           break;
//       case 9:
//           textLabel.setText(R.string.expenses);
//           detailTextLabel.setText(String.format("%.0f",
//           _property.getExpenses()));
//           break;
//       case 10:
//           textLabel.setText(R.string.rent);
//           detailTextLabel.setText(String.format("%.0f",
//           _property.getRent()));
//           break;
//
```

```
//        default:
//           break;
//        }
//     }
//
//     return view;
//   }
//
//   @Override
//   public int getCount() {
//     return 11; // 2 section + 9 fields
//   }
//
//   @Override
//   public long getItemId(int pos) {
//     return pos; // not used
//   }
//
//   @Override
//   public Object getItem(int pos) {
//     TextView textLabel = (TextView) getView(pos, null, null).
//     findViewById(R.id.textLabel);
//     if (textLabel == null) {
//       return null;
//     } else {
//       TextView detailTextLabel = (TextView) getView(pos,
//       null, null).findViewById(R.id.detailTextLabel);
//       NameValuePair nvp = new BasicNameValuePair(textLabel.
//       getText().toString(), detailTextLabel.getText().
//       toString());
//       return nvp;
//     }
//   }
// };
//}
  // android adapter to iOS datasource
  override func numberOfSectionsInTableView(tableView: UITableView) -> Int {
    return 2
  }

  override func tableView(tableView: UITableView, titleForHeaderInSection
section: Int) -> String? {
    if section == 0 {
      return NSLocalizedString("mortgage", comment: "")
    } else {
      return NSLocalizedString("operations", comment: "")
    }
  }
```

```swift
override func tableView(tableView: UITableView, numberOfRowsInSection
section: Int) -> Int {
   if section == 0 {
     return 7
   } else {
     return 2
   }
}

override func tableView(tableView: UITableView, cellForRowAtIndexPath
indexPath: NSIndexPath) -> UITableViewCell {
    var cell = tableView.dequeueReusableCellWithIdentifier("aCell",
forIndexPath: indexPath) as UITableViewCell
    var textLabel = cell.textLabel!
    var detailTextLabel = cell.detailTextLabel!

    var pos = indexPath.row
    var section = indexPath.section

    if section == 0 {
      pos = indexPath.row + 1
    } else { // 1
      pos = indexPath.row + 9
    }

    switch (pos) {
    case 1:
      textLabel.text = NSLocalizedString("purchasePrice",
      comment: "")
      detailTextLabel.text = NSString(format: "%.0f", _property.
      getPurchasePrice());
    case 2:
      textLabel.text = NSLocalizedString("downPayment", comment:
      "")

      if (_property.getPurchasePrice() > 0) {
        var down = (1 - _property.getLoanAmt() / _property.
        getPurchasePrice()) * 100.0;
        detailTextLabel.text = NSString(format: "%.0f", down);

        if (_property.getLoanAmt() == 0 && down > 0) {
          _property.setLoanAmt(_property.getPurchasePrice() *
          (1 - down / 100.0));
        }
      } else {
        detailTextLabel.text = "0";
      }
```

```
    case 3:
      textLabel.text = NSLocalizedString("loanAmount", comment: "")
      detailTextLabel.text = NSString(format: "%.2f", _property.
      getLoanAmt())
    case 4:
      textLabel.text = NSLocalizedString("interestRate", comment:
      "")
      detailTextLabel.text = NSString(format: "%.3f", _property.
      getInterestRate())
    case 5:
      textLabel.text = NSLocalizedString("mortgageTerm",
      comment: "")
      detailTextLabel.text = NSString(format: "%d", _property.
      getNumOfTerms())
    case 6:
      textLabel.text = NSLocalizedString("escrowAmount",
      comment: "")
      detailTextLabel.text = NSString(format: "%.0f",
      _property.getEscrow())
    case 7:
      textLabel.text = NSLocalizedString("extraPayment",
      comment: "")
      detailTextLabel.text = NSString(format: "%.0f",
      _property.getExtra());
    case 9:
      textLabel.text = NSLocalizedString("expenses", comment: "")
      detailTextLabel.text = NSString(format: "%.0f",
      _property.getExpenses());
    case 10:
      textLabel.text = NSLocalizedString("rent", comment: "")
      detailTextLabel.text = NSString(format: "%.0f",
      _property.getRent());

    default:
      break;
    }

    return cell
  }
  ...
}
```

3. `RentalPropertyViewController` presents `EditTextViewController` with text for editing (see Listing 5-22):

   a. Use `performSegueWithIdentifier(...)` and `prepareForSegue(...)` for screen transition and passing data to `EditTextViewController` (see Chapter 3, "Pass Data with a Segue," for detailed instructions).

   b. To return data to the presented view controller, the conventional delegate pattern works both in Android and iOS.

Listing 5-22. Present `EditTextViewController`

```
class RentalPropertyViewController : UITableViewController {
  ...
  override func tableView(tableView: UITableView, didSelectRowAtIndexPath
indexPath: NSIndexPath) {
// ((MainActivity) getActivity()).pushViewController(toFrag, true);
    self.performSegueWithIdentifier("EditText", sender: indexPath)
  }

  override func prepareForSegue(segue: UIStoryboardSegue, sender:
AnyObject?) {
    var identifier = segue.identifier
    if identifier == "EditText" {
     var indexPath = sender as NSIndexPath

   // if (position == 0 || position == 8) {
   //    return; // position 0 and 8 are header
   // }
   // EditTextViewFragment toFrag = new EditTextViewFragment();
     var toFrag =  (segue.destinationViewController as
     UINavigationController).topViewController as EditTextViewController
   // NameValuePair data = (NameValuePair) mAdapter.getItem(position);
     var cell = tableView.cellForRowAtIndexPath(indexPath)!
     var row = indexPath.row
     var section = indexPath.section
   // toFrag.setEditTextTag(position);
   // toFrag.setHeader(data.getName());
   // toFrag.setText(data.getValue());
   // toFrag.setDelegate(this);
     toFrag.editTextTag = (section == 0) ? row + 1 : row + 9
     toFrag.header = cell.textLabel!.text!
     toFrag.text = cell.detailTextLabel!.text!
     toFrag.delegate = self
   }
 }
```

```
//// delegate interface
  func onTextEditSaved(tag: Int, text: String) {
//  ((MainActivity) getActivity()).popViewController();
    self.dismissViewControllerAnimated(true, completion: nil)

    switch (tag) {
    case 1:
      _property.setPurchasePrice((text as NSString).doubleValue);
//    String percent = ((NameValuePair) mAdapter.getItem(2)).getValue();
      var indexPath = (tag < 9) ? NSIndexPath(forRow: tag - 1, inSection: 0)
: NSIndexPath(forRow: tag - 9, inSection: 1)
      var percent = tableView.cellForRowAtIndexPath(indexPath)!.
      detailTextLabel!.text!
      var down = (percent as NSString).doubleValue
      if (_property.getPurchasePrice() > 0 && _property.getLoanAmt() == 0 &&
      down > 0) {
        _property.setLoanAmt(_property.getPurchasePrice() * (1 - down /
        100.0));
      }

      break;
    case 2:
      var percentage = (text as NSString).doubleValue / 100.0;
      _property.setLoanAmt(_property.getPurchasePrice() * (1 - percentage));
      break;
    case 3:
      _property.setLoanAmt((text as NSString).doubleValue);
      break;
    case 4:
      _property.setInterestRate((text as NSString).doubleValue);
      break;
    case 5:
      _property.setNumOfTerms((text as NSString).integerValue);
      break;
    case 6:
      _property.setEscrow((text as NSString).doubleValue);
      break;
    case 7:
      _property.setExtra((text as NSString).doubleValue);
      break;
    case 9:
      _property.setExpenses((text as NSString).doubleValue);
      break;
    case 10:
      _property.setRent((text as NSString).doubleValue);
      break;

    default:
      break;
    }
```

```
    tableView.reloadData() // mAdapter.notifyDataSetChanged();
    _property.save(/* getActivity() */);
}

func onTextEditCanceled() {
//  ((MainActivity) getActivity()).popViewController();
    self.dismissViewControllerAnimated(true, completion: nil)
}
...
```

Every method is translated except doAmortization(). This method touches two common topics: RESTful Service and Saving Data (see Chapter 4). You will do this later.

Build and run the Swift project to test your code. When the Table View Cell is selected, it presents the EditTextViewController with the title and the text of the selected field for editing. After editing is done, the modified text is sent into the presenting RentalPropertyViewController via delegate and the new text is updated on the TableViewCell.

AmortizationViewController

Move on to the AmortizationViewController. It needs to render the amortization items. Do the following to port the Java implementation from Android to iOS Swift:

1. Translate the commented Java code to Swift (see Listing 5-23).

   a. Port Android Fragment life cycles to iOS View life cycles.

   b. Convert the Android BaseAdapter to iOS DataSource and delegate methods.

   c. Present MonthlyTermViewController.

Listing 5-23. EditTextViewController Life Cycle Callbacks

```
class AmortizationViewController : UITableViewController {

    var monthlyTerms: NSArray!

    override func viewDidLoad() {
//      super.onCreate(savedInstanceState);
//      mAdapter = new BaseAdapter() {
//          ...
//      };
//      this.setListAdapter(mAdapter);
        super.viewDidLoad()
    }
```

```
    override func tableView(tableView: UITableView, numberOfRowsInSection
section: Int) -> Int {
// @Override public int getCount() {
//    return monthlyTerms.length();
// }
    return monthlyTerms.count
  }


  override func tableView(tableView: UITableView, cellForRowAtIndexPath
    indexPath: NSIndexPath) -> UITableViewCell {
// @Override public View getView(int pos, View view, ViewGroup parent) {
//    if (view == null) {
//      view = getActivity().getLayoutInflater().inflate(...);
//    }
//    TextView textLabel = (TextView) view.findViewById(...);
//    TextView detailTextLabel = (TextView) view.findViewById(...);
//
//    JSONObject monthlyTerm =(JSONObject)monthlyTerms.opt(pos);
//    int pmtNo = monthlyTerm.optInt("pmtNo");
//    double balance0 = monthlyTerm.optDouble("balance0");
//    textLabel.setText(String.format("%d\t$%.2f", pmtNo, balance0));
//
//    double interest = monthlyTerm.optDouble("interest");
//    double principal = monthlyTerm.optDouble("principal");
//    detailTextLabel.setText(String.format("Interest: %.2f\tPrincipal:
%.2f", interest, principal));
//    return view;
// }
    var cell = tableView.dequeueReusableCellWithIdentifier("aCell") as
UITableViewCell!
    var textLabel = cell.textLabel!
    var detailTextLabel = cell.detailTextLabel!
    var pos = indexPath.row
    var monthlyTerm = monthlyTerms[pos] as NSDictionary
    var pmtNo = monthlyTerm["pmtNo"] as Int
    var balance0 = monthlyTerm["balance0"] as Double
    textLabel.text = NSString(format: "%d\t$%.2f", pmtNo, balance0)

    var interest = monthlyTerm["interest"] as Double
    var principal = monthlyTerm["principal"] as Double
    detailTextLabel.text = NSString(format: "Interest: %.2f\tPrincipal:
%.2f", interest, principal);

    return cell
  }


  override func viewDidAppear(animated: Bool) {
// super.onResume();
// ((MainActivity) getActivity()).slideIn(...);
// getActivity().setTitle(getText(...));
```

```
       super.viewDidAppear(animated)
       self.navigationItem.title = NSLocalizedString("label_Amortization",
   comment: "")
   }

// public void onListItemClick(...) {
//    MonthlyTermViewFragment toFrag = new MonthlyTermViewFragment();
//    JSONObject jo = (JSONObject) mAdapter.getItem(position);
//    toFrag.setMonthlyTerm(jo);
//    ((MainActivity)getActivity()).pushViewController(toFrag);
// }
   override func tableView(tableView: UITableView, didSelectRowAtIndexPath
   indexPath: NSIndexPath) {
       self.performSegueWithIdentifier("MonthlyTerm", sender: indexPath)
   }

   override func prepareForSegue(segue: UIStoryboardSegue, sender:
   AnyObject?) {
       var vc = segue.destinationViewController as MonthlyTermViewController
       var row = (sender! as NSIndexPath).row
       vc.monthlyTerm = monthlyTerms[row] as NSDictionary
   }
}
```

This completes the whole `AmortizationViewController` Swift class
implementation.

MonthlyTermViewController

Move on to the `MonthlyTermViewController`. It needs to render the
detailed info for the selected month. Do the following to port the Java
implementation from Android to iOS Swift as shown in Listing 5-24:

1. Port Android Fragment life cycles to iOS View life
   cycles.

2. Convert the Android `BaseAdapter` to iOS `DataSource`
   and implement the delegate methods.

Listing 5-24. MonthlyTermViewController Life Cycle Callbacks

```
class MonthlyTermViewController : UITableViewController {
   ...
// @Override public View onCreateView(...) {
//    contentView = inflater.inflate(...e);
//
```

```
//    mPaymentNo = (TextView)contentView.findViewById(...);
//    mTotalPmt = (TextView)contentView.findViewById(...);
//    mPrincipal = (TextView)contentView.findViewById(...);
//    mInterest = (TextView)contentView.findViewById(...);
//    mEscrow = (TextView)contentView.findViewById(...);
//    mAddlPmt = (TextView)contentView.findViewById(...);
//    mBalance = (TextView)contentView.findViewById(...);
//    mEquity = (TextView)contentView.findViewById(...);
//    mCashInvested = (TextView)contentView.findViewById(...);
//    mRoi = (TextView)contentView.findViewById(...);
//
//    double principal = this.monthlyTerm["principal"];
//    double interest = this.monthlyTerm["interest"];
//    double escrow = this.monthlyTerm["escrow"];
//    double extra = this.monthlyTerm["extra"];
//    double balance = this.monthlyTerm["balance0"] - principal;
//    int paymentPeriod = this.monthlyTerm.optInt("pmtNo");
//    double totalPmt = principal + interest + escrow + extra;
//    this.mTotalPmt.setText(String.format("$%.2f", totalPmt));
//    this.mPaymentNo.setText(String.format("No. %d", paymentPeriod));
//    this.mPrincipal.setText(String.format("$%.2f", principal));
//    this.mInterest.setText(String.format("$%.2f", interest));
//    this.mEscrow.setText(String.format("$%.2f", escrow));
//    this.mAddlPmt.setText(String.format("$%.2f", extra));
//    this.mBalance.setText(String.format("$%.2f", balance));
//
//    RentalProperty property = RentalProperty.sharedInstance();
//    double invested = property.getPurchasePrice() - property.getLoanAmt() +
      property.getExtra() * paymentPeriod;
//    double net = property.getRent() - escrow - interest - property.
      getExpenses();
//    double roi = net * 12 / invested;
//
//    this.mEquity.setText(String.format("$%.2f", property.getPurchasePrice()
      - balance));
//    this.mCashInvested.setText(String.format("$%.2f", invested));
//    this.mRoi.setText(String.format("%.2f%% ($%.2f/mo)", roi * 100, net));
//    return contentView;
// }
  override func viewDidLoad() {
    super.viewDidLoad()
    var principal = self.monthlyTerm["principal"] as Double
    var interest = self.monthlyTerm["interest"] as Double
    var escrow = self.monthlyTerm["escrow"] as Double
    var extra = self.monthlyTerm["extra"] as Double
    var balance = (self.monthlyTerm["balance0"] as Double) - principal
    var paymentPeriod = self.monthlyTerm["pmtNo"] as Int
```

```
    var totalPmt = principal + interest + escrow + extra
    self.mTotalPmt.text = NSString(format: "$%.2f", totalPmt)
    self.mPaymentNo.text = NSString(format: "No. %d", paymentPeriod)
    self.mPrincipal.text = NSString(format: "$%.2f", principal)
    self.mInterest.text = NSString(format: "$%.2f", interest)
    self.mEscrow.text = NSString(format: "$%.2f", escrow)
    self.mAddlPmt.text = NSString(format: "$%.2f", extra)
    self.mBalance.text = NSString(format: "$%.2f", balance)

    var property = RentalProperty.sharedInstance();
    var invested = property.getPurchasePrice() - property.getLoanAmt() +
    (property.getExtra() * Double(paymentPeriod))
    var net = property.getRent() - escrow - interest - property.
    getExpenses();
    var roi = net * 12 / invested

    self.mEquity.text = NSString(format: "$%.2f", property.
    getPurchasePrice() - balance)
    self.mCashInvested.text = NSString(format: "$%.2f", invested)
    self.mRoi.text = NSString(format: "%.2f%% ($%.2f/mo)", roi * 100, net)
  }

  override func viewDidAppear(animated: Bool) {
// super.onResume();
// ((MainActivity) getActivity()).slideIn(contentView, MainActivity.SLIDE_
LEFT);
// getActivity().setTitle(getText(R.string...));

    super.viewDidAppear(animated)
  }
  ...
```

This completes the whole `MonthlyTermViewController` Swift class
implementation.

RESTful Service and Saving Data

Back to the `RentalPropertyViewController`—when the "Schedule"
`UIBarButtonItem` is selected, the iOS app does the following:

1. Checks if the amortization schedule is already saved
    locally.

2. If there is no schedule found in local storage, it calls
    a remote RESTful service to get the schedules and
    save them in local storage.

3. Presents the `AmortizationViewController`, which
    renders the schedules in it in content view.

The preceding Android code was previously copied into your iOS doAmortization() method. Your mission is to translate this method to Java code, as shown in Listing 5-25.

Listing 5-25. doAmortization(...)

```
  private func doAmortization() {
// _savedAmortization = _property.getSavedAmortization(getActivity());
// if (_savedAmortization != null) {
//   AmortizationViewFragment toFrag = new AmortizationViewFragment();
//   toFrag.setMonthlyTerms(_savedAmortization);
//   ((MainActivity) getActivity()).pushViewController(toFrag, true);
// } else {
//   String url = String.format(URL_service_tmpl, _property.getLoanAmt(),
     _property.getInterestRate(), _property.getNumOfTerms(), _property.
     getExtra(), _property.getEscrow());
//   getActivity().setProgressBarIndeterminate(true);
//   getActivity().setProgressBarVisibility(true);
//
//   AsyncTask<String, Float, JSONObject> task = new AsyncTask<String,
     Float, JSONObject>() {
//     @Override
//     protected JSONObject doInBackground(String... params) {
//       String getUrl = params[0];
//       InputStream in = null;
//       HttpURLConnection conn = null;
//
//       JSONObject jo = new JSONObject();
//       try {
//         URL url = new URL(getUrl);
//         // create an HttpURLConnection by openConnection
//         conn = (HttpURLConnection) url.openConnection();
//         conn.setRequestMethod("GET");
//         conn.setRequestProperty("accept", "application/json");
//
//         int rc = conn.getResponseCode(); // HTTP status code
//         String rm = conn.getResponseMessage(); // HTTP response message.
//         Log.d("d", String.format("HTTP GET: %d %s", rc, rm));
//
//         // read message body from connection InputStream
//         in = conn.getInputStream();
//         StringBuilder builder = new StringBuilder();
//         InputStreamReader reader = new InputStreamReader(in);
//         char[] buffer = new char[1024];
//         int length;
//         while ((length = reader.read(buffer)) != -1) {
//             builder.append(buffer, 0, length);
//         }
```

```
//          in.close();
//
//          String httpBody = builder.toString();
//          jo.put(KEY_DATA, httpBody);
//
//       } catch (Exception e) {
//          e.printStackTrace();
//          try {
//             jo.putOpt(KEY_ERROR, e);
//          } catch (JSONException e1) {
//             e1.printStackTrace();
//          }
//       } finally {
//          conn.disconnect();
//       }
//       return jo;
//    }
//
//    @Override
//    protected void onPostExecute(JSONObject jo) {
//       getActivity().setProgressBarVisibility(false);
//       Exception error = (Exception) jo.opt(KEY_ERROR);
//       String errMsg = null;
//       if (error == null) {
//          AmortizationViewFragment toFrag = new AmortizationViewFragment();
//          String data = jo.optString(KEY_DATA);
//          _property.saveAmortization(data, getActivity());
//
//          try {
//             toFrag.setMonthlyTerms(new JSONArray(data));
//             ((MainActivity) getActivity()).pushViewController(toFrag, true);
//             return;
//          } catch (JSONException e) {
//             e.printStackTrace();
//             errMsg = e.getMessage();
//          }
//       } else {
//          errMsg = error.getMessage();
//       }
//       Toast.makeText(getActivity(), errMsg, Toast.LENGTH_LONG).show();
//    }
//  };
//  task.execute(url);
// }
...
```

Saving Data

In the Android RentalPropertyViewFragment.doAmortization(...), the code for saving and retrieving data is delegated to the RentalProperty model class. This uses SharedPreferences, which should be translated to iOS NSUserDefaults (see Chapter 4, "NSUserDefaults"). Do the following:

1. Use NSUserDefaults to create the following utility methods in RentalProperty.swift methods as shown in Listing 5-26.

Listing 5-26. Porting RentalProperty Save Data Utility Methods

```
class RentalProperty {
  ...
  let userDefaults = NSUserDefaults.standardUserDefaults()
  func saveUserdefault(data:AnyObject, forKey:String) -> Bool{
    userDefaults.setObject(data, forKey: forKey)
    return userDefaults.synchronize()
  }

  func retrieveUserdefault(key: String) -> AnyObject? {
    var obj: AnyObject? = userDefaults.objectForKey(key)
    return obj
  }

  func deleteUserDefault(key: String) {
    self.userDefaults.removeObjectForKey(key)
  }
  ...
```

2. Translate the load() method that loads the saved RentalProperty object from storage, as shown in Listing 5-27.

Listing 5-27. Loading RentalProperty Object from Storage

```
class RentalProperty {
  ...
// public boolean load(Context activity) {
//    String jostr = retrieveSharedPref(KEY_PROPERTY, activity);
//    if(jostr == null) {
//      return false;
//    }
//
//    try {
//      JSONObject jo = new JSONObject(jostr);
```

```
//    this.purchasePrice = jo.getDouble("purchasePrice");
//    this.loanAmt = jo.getDouble("loanAmt");
//    this.interestRate = jo.getDouble("interestRate");
//    this.numOfTerms = jo.getInt("numOfTerms");
//    this.escrow = jo.getDouble("escrow");
//    this.extra = jo.getDouble("extra");
//    this.expenses = jo.getDouble("expenses");
//    this.rent = jo.getDouble("rent");
//    return true;
//  } catch (JSONException e) {
//    e.printStackTrace();
//    return false;
//  }
// }
  func load() -> Bool {
    var data = retrieveUserdefault(MyStatic.KEY_PROPERTY) as
    NSDictionary?
    if var jo = data {
      self.purchasePrice = jo["purchasePrice"] as Double
      self.loanAmt = jo["loanAmt"] as Double
      self.interestRate = jo["interestRate"] as Double
      self.numOfTerms = jo["numOfTerms"] as Int
      self.escrow = jo["escrow"] as Double
      self.extra = jo["extra"] as Double
      self.expenses = jo["expenses"] as Double
      self.rent = jo["rent"] as Double
      return true;

    } else {
      return false
    }
  }
  ...
```

3. Translate the save() method that persists the
    RentalProperty instance in storage as shown in
    Listing 5-28.

Listing 5-28. Saving RentalProperty Object

```
class RentalProperty {
   ...
// public boolean save(Context activity) {
//    JSONObject jo = new JSONObject();
//    try {
//      jo.put("purchasePrice", purchasePrice);
//      jo.put("loanAmt", loanAmt);
//      jo.put("interestRate", interestRate);
```

```
//      jo.put("numOfTerms", numOfTerms);
//      jo.put("escrow", escrow);
//      jo.put("extra", extra);
//      jo.put("expenses", expenses);
//      jo.put("rent", rent);
//    } catch (JSONException e) {
//      e.printStackTrace();
//    }
//    return this.saveSharedPref(KEY_PROPERTY, jo.toString(),
      activity);
// }
   func save() -> Bool {
     var jo : [NSObject : AnyObject] = [
       "purchasePrice": purchasePrice,
       "loanAmt" : loanAmt,
       "interestRate" : interestRate,
       "numOfTerms" : Double(numOfTerms),
       "escrow" : escrow,
       "extra" : extra,
       "expenses" : expenses,
       "rent" : rent]

     return self.saveUserdefault(jo, forKey: MyStatic.KEY_
     PROPERTY)
   }
   ...
```

4. Translate the getSavedAmortization() method
    that retrieves the amortization schedule array from
    storage as shown in Listing 5-29.

Listing 5-29. Retrieve Amortization Schedule Array from Persistent Storage

```
class RentalProperty {
   ...
// public JSONArray getSavedAmortization(Context activity) {
//   String savedKey = retrieveSharedPref(KEY_AMO_SAVED, activity);
//   String aKey = this.getAmortizationPersistentKey();
//   if(savedKey.length() > 0 && savedKey.equals(aKey)) {
//     String jsonArrayString = retrieveSharedPref(savedKey, activity);
//     try {
//       return new JSONArray(jsonArrayString);
//     } catch (JSONException e) {
//       return null;
//     }
//   } else {
//     return null;
//   }
// }
```

```
func getSavedAmortization() -> NSArray? {
  var savedKey = retrieveUserdefault(MyStatic.KEY_AMO_SAVED) as String?
  var aKey = self.getAmortizationPersistentKey()
  if let str = savedKey {
    if(str.utf16Count > 0 && str == aKey) {
      var jo = retrieveUserdefault(str) as NSArray?
      return jo
    }
  }
  return nil
}
...
```

5. Translate the saveAmortization() method that persists the amortization schedule array as shown in Listing 5-30.

Listing 5-30. Persist Amortization Schedule Array

```
class RentalProperty {
...
// public boolean saveAmortization(String data, Context activity) {
//    String aKey = this.getAmortizationPersistentKey();
//    saveSharedPref(KEY_AMO_SAVED, aKey, activity);
//    saveSharedPref(aKey, data, activity);
// }
  func saveAmortization(data: NSArray) -> Bool {
    var aKey = self.getAmortizationPersistentKey()
    saveUserdefault(aKey, forKey: MyStatic.KEY_AMO_SAVED)
    return saveUserdefault(data, forKey: aKey)
  }
...
```

6. Translate the rest of the commented Java code to Swift as shown in Listing 5-31. Swift static variables are always lazily initialized. Unlike in Java, you don't need to do null check in the sharedInstance() method.

Listing 5-31. Miscellaneous Methods in RentalProperty Model

```
class RentalProperty {
...
// public static RentalProperty sharedInstance() {
//    if (_sharedInstance == null) {
//      _sharedInstance = new RentalProperty();
//    }
//    return _sharedInstance;
// }
```

```
class func sharedInstance() -> RentalProperty {
  return MyStatic._sharedInstance
}

// public String getAmortizationPersistentKey() {
//    String aKey = String.format("%.2f-%.3f-%d-%.2f", this.loanAmt, this.
interestRate, this.numOfTerms, this.extra);
//    return aKey;
// }
  func getAmortizationPersistentKey() -> String {
    var aKey = String(format: "%.2f-%.3f-%d-%.2f", self.loanAmt, self.
interestRate, self.numOfTerms, self.extra);
    return aKey;
  }
  ...
```

You have ported the "save data" code and the whole RentalProperty model class from the Android app.

Use RESTful Service

Recall the doAmortization() method—it performs remote operations in the background, then updates the UI when data is returned. The Android counterpart uses AsyncTask and HttpURLConnection to accomplish this task (see Listing 5-25). In iOS, use the instructions in the "NSURLConnection" section in Chapter 4 to do the following:

1. To pass data to the presented AmortizationViewController from the presenting RentalPropertyViewController, call performSegueWithIdentifier(...) and prepareForSegue(...).

2. To get data from a remote RESTFul service, use iOS's NSURLConnection.sendAsynchronousRequest to replace the Android AsyncTask+ HttpURLConnection as shown in Listing 5-32.

Listing 5-32. Using RentalPropertyViewController to Pass Data to the Presented AmortizationViewController

```
class RentalProperty {
  ...
  override func prepareForSegue(segue: UIStoryboardSegue, sender:
AnyObject?) {
    var identifier = segue.identifier
    if identifier == "EditText" {
      ...
    } else { // AmortizationTable segue
      // AmortizationViewFragment toFrag = new AmortizationViewFragment();
      // toFrag.setMonthlyTerms(_savedAmortization);
      var toFrag = segue.destinationViewController as
AmortizationViewController
      toFrag.monthlyTerms = sender as NSArray
    }
  }

  private func doAmortization() {
    _savedAmortization = _property.getSavedAmortization();
    if (_savedAmortization != nil) {
      performSegueWithIdentifier("AmortizationTable", sender: _
savedAmortization!)
    } else {
      var url = NSString(format: MyStatic.URL_service_tmpl, _property.
      getLoanAmt(), _property.getInterestRate(), _property.getNumOfTerms(),
      _property.getExtra(), _property.getEscrow())
      UIApplication.sharedApplication().networkActivityIndicatorVisible =
      true

      var urlRequest = NSMutableURLRequest(URL: NSURL(string: url)!)
      urlRequest.HTTPMethod = "GET"
      urlRequest.setValue("text/html",forHTTPHeaderField: "accept")
      NSURLConnection.sendAsynchronousRequest(urlRequest, queue:
      NSOperationQueue.mainQueue(),
        completionHandler: {(resp: NSURLResponse!, data: NSData!, error:
        NSError!) -> Void in
          NSURLConnection.sendAsynchronousRequest(urlRequest,
          queue: NSOperationQueue.mainQueue(),
            completionHandler: {(resp: NSURLResponse!, data: NSData!,
            error: NSError!) -> Void in
              UIApplication.sharedApplication().
              networkActivityIndicatorVisible = false
              var errMsg: String?
              if error == nil {
                var statusCode = (resp as NSHTTPURLResponse).statusCode
                if(statusCode == 200) {
                  var str = NSString(data: data, encoding: NSUTF8StringEncoding)
```

```
                var parseErr: NSError?
                var json = NSJSONSerialization.JSONObjectWithData(data,
    options: NSJSONReadingOptions.AllowFragments, error: &parseErr) as NSArray?
                if parseErr == nil {
                    self._property.saveAmortization(json!)
                    self.performSegueWithIdentifier("AmortizationTable",
                    sender: json!)
                    return
                } else {
                    errMsg = parseErr?.debugDescription
                }
            } else {
                errMsg = "HTTP RC: \(statusCode)"
            }
        } else {
            errMsg = error.debugDescription
        }

        // show error
        var alert = UIAlertController(title: "Error", message: errMsg,
        preferredStyle: UIAlertControllerStyle.Alert)
        var actionCancel = UIAlertAction(title: "Cancel", style:
        UIAlertActionStyle.Cancel,
          handler: {action in
            // do nothing
        })
        alert.addAction(actionCancel)
        self.presentViewController(alert, animated: true,
        completion: nil)
    })
  })
 }
}
...
```

All the class translations are completed. Build and run the iOS RentalROI app to make sure it behaves the same as the Android app. I normally put the iOS and Android apps side by side for testing. Even for testing activities, it takes less time to test iOS and Android apps in parallel. Figure 5-12 shows the iOS version in action.

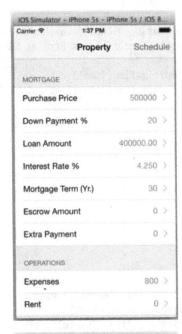

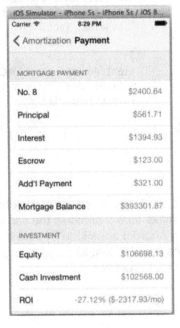

Figure 5-12. The completed iOS RentalROI app

Summary

This chapter intended to show how to port the whole app, end to end, by applying the individual mapping topics introduced in Chapters 3 and 4, such as the master list details drill-down, navigation patterns, basic UI widgets, saving data, and using remote services.

You started by using the storyboard to create MVC components and using storyboard segues to connect the View Controller together. The result was a set of connected View Controllers.

You continued to drill down into each class, one by one, starting by translating all the members' declarations for all the classes first. Then, you drilled down into each method. Translating expressions in each method was generally straightforward. Using a global find-and-replace makes this type of translation quick and fun. When you encounter platform-specific SDK or topics, use this book's Table of Contents to find the instructions that will guide you through your porting efforts.

As you port an app, you will start to see more searchable and replaceable patterns. I use the Xcode editor's **Find and Replace All** one click at a time, so that I can have a quick read on the code being replaced. Learning is the main objective in your early iOS journey. Reading, typing, and debugging the code seems the best way to learn a new programming language.

Although the `RentalROI` app is not complicated enough to show you more advanced topics that are not included in this book, the porting steps remain the same: you always break the app down into the smallest porting components possible—a single line of expression, a method, or sometimes an entire class or even a common use case. This porting strategy always works for me.

Index

W

X, Y, Z

Get the eBook for only $10!

Now you can take the weightless companion with you anywhere, anytime. Your purchase of this book entitles you to 3 electronic versions for only $10.

This Apress title will prove so indispensible that you'll want to carry it with you everywhere, which is why we are offering the eBook in 3 formats for only $10 if you have already purchased the print book.

Convenient and fully searchable, the PDF version enables you to easily find and copy code—or perform examples by quickly toggling between instructions and   applications. The MOBI format is ideal for your Kindle, while the ePUB can be utilized on a variety of mobile devices.

Go to www.apress.com/promo/tendollars to purchase your companion eBook.

Apress®
THE EXPERT'S VOICE™